The Book of Esther
God Watches from the Shadows

J. Thomas Ruble II

THE BOOK OF ESTHER
GOD WATCHES FROM THE SHADOWS

J. THOMAS RUBLE II

The Book of Esther: God Watches from the Shadows
by J. Thomas Ruble II
Copyright © 2023 by Jeffrey Thomas Ruble II
All Rights Reserved.
ISBN: 978-1-59755-729-0

Published by: ADVANTAGE BOOKS™, Longwood, FL, www.advbookstore.com

All Rights Reserved. This book and parts thereof may not be reproduced in any form, stored in a retrieval system or transmitted in any form by any means (electronic, mechanical, photocopy, recording or otherwise) without prior written permission of the author, except as provided by United States of America copyright law.

Scriptures are taken from the Holy Bible NEW KING JAMES VERSION®. (NKJV) Copyright© 1982 by Thomas Nelson, Inc. Used by permission. All rights reserved.

Library of Congress Catalog Number: 2023937156

Name:	Ruble II, J. Thomas, Author
Title:	*The Book of Esther: God Watches from the Shadows*
	J. Thomas Ruble II
	Advantage Books, 2023
Identifiers:	ISBN Paperback: 978159757290
Subjects:	Christian Life - Inspirational
	Bible Study - Old Testament

First Printing: June 2023
23 24 25 26 27 28   10 9 8 7 6 5 4 3 2 1

Table of Contents

INTRODUCTION 7

1: RASH DECISION OF A DRUNK KING 11

2: PROVINCE BEAUTY PAGEANT 31

3: PROMOTION OF A WICKED MAN 53

4: EVIL PLANS OF A WICKED MAN REVEALED 71

5: ESTHER TO THE RESCUE 89

6: GOD REVEALS HIS PLAN WITH A SENSE OF HUMOR 105

7: LAST MEAL, SUDDEN DEATH 121

8: GOD'S REVERSAL OF WICKED PLANS 135

9: GREAT CELEBRATION OF THE FEAST OF PURIM 151

10: PEACE & PROSPERITY 167

J. Thomas Ruble II

Introduction

There are sixty-six books in the Bible. Out of those sixty-six books two of them bare the names of women. The first one, is named after Ruth, who was a Moabite, from the land of Moab. The second book is named after Esther, who was a Hebrew young woman, who became queen in the land of Persia.

This book is very interesting, because God is never mentioned in any of the ten chapters that makes up this book. Although His name is never mentioned in this book, we can see that His name is silent; but His will and work is being performed in the life of His people Israel.

The author of this book is unknown. Some say that it could have been, Ezra, Nehemiah, or could have possibly been Mordecai, Esther's cousin. J. Vernon McGee brought up an interesting point in his commentary, based off Esther 9:20, that Mordecai wrote this book. "And Mordecai wrote these things and sent letters to all the Jews, near and far, who were in all the provinces of King Ahasuerus," It could have very possible that he is right. However, I myself decline to speculate about who it was that wrote this book. To me we just do not have any idea who wrote it. But we are to leave these things up to God about who wrote it. For it was He who spoke these words to someone. He knows who wrote it and that is all that's matters.

According to the Matthew Henry Study Bible. The events of this book took place during the exile of the Jews between 483 to 471 B.C. This was between the first return under Zerrubbal 537 B.C. and the later returns under Ezra 458 B.C. and Nehemiah 444 B.C.

Several commentaries as well as J. Vernon McGee Commentary on Esther states that the Name of God is never mentioned in this book. But each on also stated that although God is not mentioned; God is in the shadows watching over His people and working out His providence through His people.

Matthew Henry Commentary that stated that prayer was not even mentioned in this book. Only fasting was mentioned. J. Vernon McGee also stated that prayer was not mentioned in this book either. However, we will learn that the two fasting and praying go together.

At this point all the Jews had not returned to their homeland in Israel, Judah and Jerusalem. In 538 B.C. King Cyrus gave the Jews the right to return to

Judah to rebuild the temple in Jerusalem. There was only around 50,000 exiled Jews who had returned to Jerusalem, to rebuild the walls and the temple.

I meditated on this for several days, of why they did not return to Israel as God had commanded them to do. As I thought on these things, I remembered scripture from Jeremiah 29:4-7; when Jeremiah had spoken these words to those in Babylonian captivity.

> ***"Thus says the Lord of hosts, the God of Israel, to all who were carried away captive, whom I have caused to be carried away from Jerusalem to Babylon: Build houses and dwell in them; plant gardens and eat their fruit. Take wives and beget sons and daughters; and take wives for your sons and give your daughters to husbands, so that they may bear sons and daughters-that you may be increased there, and not diminished. And seek the peace of the city where I have caused you to be carried away captive, and pray to the Lord for it; for in its peace you will have peace."***

They were to build houses to live in, because they were going to be there for seventy years. I believe some if not all became comfortable with life while living in Babylon. Then when God sent Darius into Babylon who gave everyone the right to return to where they came from. They remained in Babylon, and some stayed in Persia to live.

There was a time when Jacob had returned from living with his Uncle Laban. That he build a house for himself, found in Genesis 33:17. But as he tarried there, disaster struck him and his family. For it was here that a young man named Shechem raped Dinah the daughter of Jacob. After this took place, they had agreed for her and Shechem to be married, if they would become circumcised as they were. They agreed to the terms, and they took Dinah with them to the City of Shechem. But while all the men were recovering from being circumcised, Simeon and Levi sought revenge for their sister and killed all the men in that city.

I don't understand it all, but Jeremiah told them that it came from God. They were to build houses, plant gardens, and marry. He wanted them to carry on with everyday life, and to not sit around being idle, crying "Woe is us!" Maybe God was testing them, to see what they would do later on once the seventy years had expired.

Introduction

The same holds true for us today. Have we become so accustomed to the ways of this world; that we've become comfortable with it's sins and pleasures? I believe that all of us have to some extent in our lives.

J. Thomas Ruble II

1

Rash Decision of a Drunk King

Verses 1-3

Now it came to pass in the days of Ahasuerus (this was the Ahasuerus who reigned over one hundred and twenty-seven provinces, from India to Ethiopia),

In those days when King Ahasuerus sat on the throne of his kingdom, which was in Shushan the citadel,

That in the third year of his reign he made a feast for all his officials and servants- the powers of Persia and Media, the nobles, and the princes of the provinces being before him-

    According to J. Vernon McGee Commentary on Esther. He says that the name Ahasuerus is not the proper name of a man, but it was a title. The name Ahasuerus means, "high father" or "venerable king." As the word Caesar is a title and does not identify the man, so Ahasuerus does not identify this Persian King in secular history. There is quite a divergence of opinion concerning his identity.

    He goes on to say, that this Ahasuerus of the Book of Esther is Xerxes the Great of Persia. For he is the one who actually brought the kingdom to it's zenith. Xerxes and Esther were the parents of Darius II (424-404 B.C.)

    From verse one we see that the extent of his kingdom is very large. He reigned over one hundred and twenty-seven provinces. A province is a function, office, or duty. It is the acts or operations expected of a person or thing. More less it is like the United States. Our overall governing body is in Washington D.C., but we are broken down by states. In these states we have governing bodies known as governors.

This was a very great area of land for one man to reign over. This was the great empire of Persia during its day. His kingdom was from the land of India, Pakistan, Afghanistan, Iraq, Syria, Jordan, Israel, Egypt, Ethiopia, Turkey, to the border of Greece. This was a total of 3 million square miles, that would be the entire size of the United States.

The city where he reigned from is called Shushan or Susa. It was 160 miles east of the Tigris River between the Karkheh and Dez Rivers in Iran. It also served as the capital of Elam. Today the modern town of Shush, Iran is located on the site of ancient Susa. (information from Wikipedia)

In verse three we see that he has reigned over they one hundred and twenty-seven provinces of three years. Which during his third year of reign that he had made a great feast through out his entire kingdom. He had invited at least two thousand people to be his guest in Susa for this party. This feast he had was for all of those who governed his vast kingdom. This would be like the President of the United States having a party for all the governors of each state and their staff. Where I am from, we'd call that a big shindig!

As we go through this book. I want you to keep in mind of the parties that this man had. Because King Ahasuerus or Xerxes was known as a party animal. He was a drunkard and a glutton. He loved rubbing elbows with those who he had placed in authority.

He was the first-born son of Darius I and his mother Atossa, the daughter of Cyrus; he was the first born to Darius after his accession to the throne. Xerxes was designated heir apparent by his father in preference to his elder brother Artabazanes. His father died, in 486 B.C., and Xerxes was about 35 years old and had already governed Babylonia at least 12 years.

One of his first concerns upon his accession was to pacify Egypt, where a usurper had been governing for two years. But he was forced to use much stronger methods than had Darius: in 484 B.C. He ravaged the Delta and chastised the Egyptians.

He had learned of a revolt of Babylon, where two nationalist pretenders had appeared in swift succession. The second Shamash-eriba, was conquered by Xerxes' son in law, and violent repression ensued: Babylon's fortresses' were torn down, its temples pillaged and the statue of Marduk destroyed. (information from Britannica.Com)

He also oversaw the completion of various construction projects left unfinished by his father at Susa and Persepolis. He oversaw the building of the Gate of All Nations and the Hall of a Hundred Columns at Persepolis, which are the largest and most imposing structures of the palace. (information from Wikipedia)

Verses 4-8

Showing Off, Bragging Rights

When he showed the riches of his glorious kingdom and the splendor of his excellent majesty for many days, one hundred and eighty in all. And when these days were completed, the king made a feast lasting seven days for all the people who were present in Shushan the citadel, from great to small, in the court of the garden of the king's palace.

There were white and blue linen curtains fastened with cords of fine linen and purple on silver rods and marble pillars; and the couches were of gold and silver on a mosaic pavement of alabaster, turquoise, and white and black marble. And they served drinks in golden vessels, each vessel being different from the other, with royal wine in abundance, according to the generosity of the king.

All of us at some point in our lives we have met people who are not very humble at all. They are showoffs, they like to strut around like a peacock. They want to show us all the things that they have and all things that we don't have.

Here in verse four, we see that King Ahasuerus is showing off for all his quest. Notice the words glorious, splendor, excellent majesty. The word glorious means having a striking beauty or splendor that evokes feelings of delighted admiration. Splendor means magnificent and splendid appearance, grandeur. The word excellent means extremely good; outstanding. And the word majesty means impressive stateliness, dignity, or beauty.

He was more less telling everyone, "look at what I have done! Look at what I have built. Is there any man that is as wealthy and rich as I am. I am king over one hundred and twenty-seven provinces."

J. Vernon McGee states in his commentary. "This banquet revealed the wealth, the luxury, and the regal character of this oriental court. As I have indicated the reason for it is obvious. He had called in all his princes and all his rulers from every corner of his kingdom that he might win their wholehearted support for the military campaign to capture Greece and to make himself the supreme ruler of the world of that day."

Where I come from, we would call that buttering them up. He has something up his sleeve. So he is showing them that he was able to afford a war against Greece. He wanted them to rest assure, to put their worries to rest that he could afford it. When you stop to think about it, we see that man has not changed at all.

I don't know the exact dollar amount that it cost him to have this feast. But I would have to say that it cost him in todays money, that it would have been one to three million dollars. The reason I say that is because this feast went on for one hundred and eighty days. This means that this feast went on for six months. Six months of drinking and eating.

Where was God? Was God invited? Apparently not because we have to realize that the Meds and Persians were pagans. They did not follow the law of God as the Jewish people did. Their laws were different. The gods they served were not gods at all, they was made of wood, stone, and probably gold.

King Ahasuerus reminds me of the Parable of the Rich Man's Barns that Jesus told. This man had a farm that produced a very large crop. Since he had a bumper crop year, this man said, "What shall I do, since I have no more room to store my crops? So, he said I will pull down my barns and build bigger barns. There I will store all my crops."

Then he said," I will say to my soul you have many goods laid up for many years, take it easy, eat drink and be merry." But God said to him, "Thou Fool! This night your soul be required of you, then whose will those things be which you have provided."

Each time I read that parable, I usually think that this man in this parable could have been Nabal. Because Nabal was a rich man who had rejected David and his men from partaking of food from his table. And also, the name Nabal means fool!

He reminds me also of Nebuchadnezzar, the king of Babylon. Daniel 4:28-37, tells us of how Nebuchadnezzar was walking around in his royal palace of

1: Rash Decision of a Drunk King

Babylon. He said, Is not this great Babylon, that I have built for a royal dwelling by my mighty power and for the honor of my Majesty?" But then a voice from heaven came to Him and said, "King Nebuchadnezzar, to you it is spoken; the kingdom has departed from you!" The next thing he knew he went stark mad out of his mind and began living with the beast of the field. He was eating grass like an ox, his body covered with the dew from heaven. His hair grew as long as the feathers of an eagle and his fingernails grew long like birds' claws. But then he looked up to heaven and he blessed the Most High and praised and honored Him who lived forever.

To tell you the truth. When I was younger, I always wanted our family to become rich. The reason why is because our dad, our mom and we kids use to work hard on the farm. We had to do without a lot of things that the other kids at school had. They had the expensive cars, clothes, shoes, and their houses were a lot bigger and had everything up to date.

We seen our dad set and cry because he couldn't afford to give us things like this. But I'll tell you something, I wouldn't take all the money, silver or gold for all the good memories of our childhood. The one thing that our parents gave us kids while growing up was priceless. They took us to church, read Bible stories, read the Bible to us, sang hymns around the piano. All four of us accepted the Lord as our Savior.

What our parents gave us is what Jesus said in Matthew 6:19-20 NKJV

"Do not lay up for yourselves treasures on earth, where moth and rust destroy and where thieves break in and steal; but lay up for yourselves treasures in heaven, where neither moth nor rust destroys and where thieves do not break in and steal."

My favorite Bible verse on this is what Jesus said, in Luke 12:15

And He said to them, "Take heed and beware of covetousness, for one's life does not consist in the abundance of the things he possesses."

King Ahasuerus may have had all these riches and all these wealthy possessions. But he could only enjoy them while he was living on this earth. There was no taking all of these riches with him when he died. Not only that but all these things would one day rot away.

Once the one hundred and eighty days was over with, he extended the feast by another week. During this time, he invited everyone else. This would have been the common folk living in Susa. I'll say one thing about him, being a rich pagan king, at least he remembered the common people. He's a better fellow than the leaders of other nations, and our nation, thumbing their noses at those who are poor and homeless.

I recall the Super Bowl that was being played one year in Los Angeles, California. They put all the homeless on buses and moved them to around town. The reason for them doing this was because they were an embarrassment to their city and the NFL. Really! Why didn't they invite them in to watch the game? Just because they moved them to another city, they were still homeless. Now they want them to be an embarrassment to another city.

Here in verse six, we are give a very descriptive picture of the beauty and wealth of King Xerxes. The curtains were white, green, and blue. They were fastened with cords of fine linen and purple to silver rings. The pillars holding up the palace was of Marble. The beds or couches were of gold and silver. The pavement that they set on was or red, blue, and white and black marble.

This detailed description reminds me of Robin Leach's show known as "The Lifestyles of the Rich and Famous." On this show he would take everyone through the mansions that the Hollywood Stars, Basketball, Football stars owned. These mansions had more rooms, beautiful marble floors, several bathrooms, indoor and outdoor swimming pools and more. Some had tennis courts, basketball courts, and hot tubs. This is the way that society measures someone's worth and success.

To those of us who live in more modest means of living, we are often awe struck by the glitter and glamour of how they live. We think that all of those people have everything in the world that they want, minus problems in life like we have. But deep down inside, nine times out of ten, these people have everything but true happiness. That's why I'd say, at least 85% of them are miserable, lonely, and depressed. They have all that wealth, but they have no peace or true happiness.

I often joke around with people I work with, as well at church or in stores we go to; I'll say, "How's all the poor people?" Some respond, "Still poor and getting poorer!" We have a good laugh about it, then I will tell them, "Well at least no one can come and take anything away from us!" Then we'll have another laugh.

It took me awhile to learn this, and I am still learning it each day. We who are Christians are the richest people living on God's green earth. Because we have been bought with the blood of Christ, Jesus Christ is our Lord and King. He has a kingdom, that makes us Prince and Princess'.

There is a Evangelist that I dearly love from yesteryear, named Vance Havner. He said, "If you are a Christian, you are not a citizen of this world trying to get to heaven; you are a citizen of heaven making your way through this world."

Now listen to me carefully, because I haven't gone from preaching to meddling! But have you ever noticed that the churches across the United States have become like the world. I mean they build these huge mega churches today with everything sparkling and shining. Everything has to be up to date, fancy, eloquent, the best that money can by. Really? Since when did all of this become part of God's plan. Don't forget when King David wanted to build a temple for God, and God told him; that He had always dwelt in a tent.

Thank God that Jesus don't accept us into His family based off our bank accounts, houses we live in or what we drive. He want's us to be rich in Him spiritually, to mature into the very Person He was. Think about it? He left ALL the SPLENDOR of heaven, to humble Himself as a slave to die for us. Philippians 2:7

In verses seven through eight, we see that he gave the people the best drinking cups that he had. This was not our everyday Dixie Cups we use at picnics. Every one of these cups were made of pure gold. Then each cup had a different design from the next cup.

Next, we see that he served them with the best wine, that came from the king's cellar. This wine was the best of the best. This wasn't your cheap wine that came in a box, like they use to have back in the 80's and 90's. This wine was the top of the line. This drinking that went on here, was ordered by the king for every person to drink their fill, the sky was the limit. This reminded me of seeing October Feast while stationed in Germany. There was drinking all you wanted to drink, eat all you wanted to eat and dance till you passed out. However, the king allowed every person in attendance to drink what they wanted, without him pressuring them to drink. Times have changed since Xerxes' days! Because today if a woman or a man are a Christian who works in the business world. They are invited to parties where there is drinking, and they are pressured into drinking. If they don't participate in the drinking as well as other sinful activities; they are frowned upon, ostracized, or threatened of losing their jobs.

I can remember times growing up in our High School years. There were times when my brother and I had peer-pressure on us. On the weekends, they tried hard to get us to drink beer or some other intoxicating beverage. Through the week, some of our friends who did speed or smoked joints offered it to us outside of class. They would tell us how it made you feel and the mighty things you could do with it. Some would let it go that we didn't want it, but we got teased a little, but they finally let it drop. Others were very persistent in offering it to us, which lead us being backed in a corner. Which then lead to raising our voices as well as our fist.

While serving in the Army at Fort Stewart, Georgia, I encountered this again. Everyone in my platoon found out that I had never once smoked weed in my life. They thought that I was lying, or that I was just joking around with them. They tried talking me into doing it, hounding me for hours. So I told them that I might try it when we get out of this field and back to garrison. From that time, I said that until the day came for our return to garrison, the Lord really worked on me. So I was hoping they'd forget about, that didn't happen. They were holding my feet to the fire about it and brought it to my room to try. It stunk! I told the young man that I didn't want to that I changed my mind. The argument built in a fury and when it did I accidently hit his hand sending the burning weed to the floor.

Needless to say, a fight ensued, with me getting the worse of it; but the next day he knew who had been there. I wish I could say that it ended there but it didn't. Everyone in the platoon except for my roommate ignored me and whispered about me. A week later, things changed. We had a Company urinalysis test done. I knew that I had nothing to worry about. But I felt bad for my buddies because I knew they were going to fail, which they did. But to my surprise, a couple of days after the test, just about all of them came and apologized to me; even the young man who fought me. He even gave me a hug and told me what a big man I was to stand up to him. After all this young man was 5'8" tall and could bench press bulldozer. Compared to me being 5'6" tall and weighed maybe 110 pounds wet. Times have really changed since Xerxes' days, as well as the time period we grew up in, times are worse than they ever have been.

1: Rash Decision of a Drunk King

So now we know a little more about King Xerxes', how he lived it up, his drinking and party's, all of his wealth and accomplishments in life. B.R. Lakin another Evangelist from yesteryear that I truly love said, "Show me how a man lives, and I'll show you how a man dies!" Later on in life he was assassinated by a bodyguard.

Next, we are going to learn about his wife the Queen, Queen Vashti verses 9-12.

A beautiful Queens Refusal

Verses 9-12

Queen Vashti also made a feast for the women in the royal palace which belonged to King Ahasuerus.

On the seventh day, when the heart of the king was merry with wine, he commanded Mehuman, Biztha, Harbona, Bigtha, Abagtha, Zethar, and Carcas, seven eunuchs who served in the presence of King Ahasuerus,

To bring Queen Vashti before the king, wearing her royal crown, in order to how her beauty to the people and the officials, for she was beautiful to behold.

But Queen Vashti refused to come at the king's command brought by his eunuchs; therefore the king was furious, and his anger burned within him.

Vashti's name means, that drinks; thread (Hitchcock's Bible Names Dictionary)

From Smiths, Easton's, International Standard Bible says her name means; Beautiful.

From the Encyclopedia. Com says that she came from Babylon. Her grandfather was Nebuchadnezzar, and her father was Belshazzar.

If you notice at the beginning of this verse, it tells us that Vashti had made a feast for the women. It has been said that in the ancient times they separated themselves like this, because they did not mix sex and business. So, she entertained the women, while the king entertained the men and talked business. These women she had at her feast would have been the wives of all the men who accompanied their husbands to this feast.

Once again, we see how the times have changed, because wives today usually travel with their husbands to business party's. Often time they do not go along with them, but the one hosting party will have escorts there to mingle with the men. Then they wonder why they get into trouble later on for sexual harassment.

But things did not happen like this during Xerxes' day. When it came to doing business the women where off by themselves doing their own thing. That is so that there would be absolutely no interfering with business. Because after all there would have been chaos with both men and women being drunk.

Then we see that the king's heart is merry with wine. In other words, he is drunk, he is ten foot tall and bullet proof. Now he has gone from talking to thinking about his beautiful queen. He would have been a good candidate, for Loretta Lynn writing, "Don't Come Home Drinking, With Loving on Your Mind."

Notice that the writer here uses the word merry which means, full of gaiety, or high spirits; marked by festivity or gaiety. Just like during Christmas time we tell each other "Merry Christmas." We're saying be full of happiness and cheer.

Well, the king here is cheerful with another spirit. He is fill with the spirit of wine. More less he is tipsy, buzzed, almost to the point of drunkenness.

The Bible tells us in Ephesians 5:18:

"And do not be drunk with wine, in which is dissipation; but be filled with the Spirit." NKJV

I really like the New Living Translation of Ephesians 5:18
"Don't be drunk with wine because that will ruin your life. Instead, be filled with the Spirit."

How many lives? How many families lives? Have been ruined because of alcohol. Alcohol has broken up more families due to their family member drinking all the time. It has led to men and women both physically and emotionally abusing their families. It has led to men and women both getting behind the wheel while intoxicated and killing someone who was innocent.

1: Rash Decision of a Drunk King

I gave you the NKJV and the NLT versions of this verse. The NKJV, uses the word dissipation, a word that means- dissipated living. This is not a word that we use very much today. So here are a few words that are similar: Debauchery, excess, self- indulgence, wildness, depravity, corruption, immorality, promiscuity.

This is where we are at today in our nation. Take a good look around you at those who once were successful women and men, who are now down on skid row, and homeless.

I recall a song written and performed by George Jones called *"Choices"* It may be a country song but there is a lot truth to that song.

King Xerxes' is the leader of one hundred and twenty-seven provinces. He is a leader, and a leader should always be sober minded for making wise decisions. Because being in a drunken stupor, it is hard to make clear decisions. So, he gives them the command to bring the queen to him, while he is drunk. This isn't going to end well folks.

Where are we at today? Are we living with ghost in our attics? Are you living with bad choices from your past? All of us at some time in our lives have made very bad choices. Romans 3:23 tells us, **"for ALL have sinned and fall short of the glory of God."** There is only ONE person who can help us with bad choices we've made and that is the Lord Jesus Christ. He was and is the Son of God. He and only He is the One who has lived on earth in a fleshly body like ours and overcame sin.

He can and will deliver us from the bad choices that we made if we will only allow Him to. Only thing is, is this; He can help us over come, but we will still have to pay for our actions. He will also walk with us and teach us how to have joy while we go through this.

In verse twelve we see that this verse brings about a turning point here for the entire setting for the book of Esther. Because when the eunuchs came to Vashti with the command of the King to come to him, wearing her crown. That this command did not set well with her at all.

Now I believe that Queen Vashti had a justified reason for not going to the king at his banquet. I believe that if she had gone that it would not have turned out very well. We are not told here in the scriptures for her reason of not going to him. But suppose that he had done this before, and it had embarrassed her.

Also, if she had gone to that banquet of all men, there would have been men whistling at her, undressing her with their eyes.

In these times they lived women were treated with disrespect and looked down upon. They were often physically mistreated. I don't know for certain that the king would have done this himself or allowed anyone else to do the same. But as drunk as they all were anything could have happened.

A married man and woman should communicate with each other and listen to each other. The Bible clearly tells us that a man is to love his wife, he is to provide for her and protect her. Look at what the Bible says in Ephesians 5:25&28,

"Husbands love your wives even as Christ also loved the church and gave Himself for it. So ought man to love their wives as their own bodies. He that love his wife love himself."

God created women for a man to be his helper. He gave them a mind, a heart a soul, feelings to love and to receive love. He gave her to a man to be someone that he could talk to, share things with, and to stand by him for moral support. He did not create them to be slapped, beat like a punching bag, ridiculed, ignored or sexually exploited.

She may not have wanted to go because there were common people there. Maybe she wasn't the type who liked the common people. If that was the case, then she should not have been like that.

There is a story that has been told that the reason she did not go was because; the king wanted her to wear nothing but the crown. But a lot of theologians believe that this story was fiction, as well as I do.

Now I also believe that in some ways she was wrong in not going to him. The reason I say this is because the Bible tells us that a wife should obey her husband. In Ephesians 5:24 the Bible says,

"Wives, submit yourselves unto your husbands, as unto the Lord."

Things have really changed for the worst in our day and time. While studying to write this I was flabbergasted in my research. They have web sites for spouses who want to cheat on their spouses. There is also a thing called swinging, or where a man will allow another man to have sex with his wife; and vice- versa. I thought to myself that we have become like Sodom and

Gomorrah. Men if you are doing this with your wife, please stop because it is sin, it is immoral. You are hurting your wife as well as yourself.

We know that this did not go over very well with the king because he was very, very angry with Vashti for disobeying him. He wasn't seething with anger, he was burning with anger. With the anger he had towards her he could have had her killed at this point.

Divorce proceedings begin

> ***Esther 1:13-15 Then the king said to the wise men who understood the times (for this was the king's manner toward all who knew law and justice,***
>
> ***Those closet to him being Carshena, Shethar, Admatha, Tarshish, Meres, Marsena, and Memucan, the sevenprinces of Persia and Media, who had access to the king's presence, and who ranked highest in the kingdom):***
>
> ***"What shall we do to Queen Vashti, according to law, because she did not obey the command of King Ahasuerus brought to her by the eunuchs?"***

After being told that Queen Vashti said, "No!" King Xerxes had to be flabbergasted in front of all the men at his banquet. He was livid. Here he is the king over a vast kingdom, throwing a party, showing off his great wealth and power. Then his wife tells him "No!" This had to make him look as if he is weak before all his guest.

Although he is very angry, he turns to his wise men who knows the laws of the Meds and Persians very well. Men of power should always ask other for advice. But men of power should always seek God and ask Him his advice over man's advice.

King David was a man for the most part who always sought God's advice on what to do. There were also several kings of Judah who sought God for advice. They went to their advisor's, to go to the prophets of their day to seek God for His word.

There were some in Judah who did not do this, while none of the kings of Israel ever sought God. Nebuchadnezzar and Belshazzar they always asked advice of men, magicians and fortune tellers. The Bible tells us,

> ***Psalm 118:8 KJV "It's better to trust in the Lord than to put confidence in man."***
>
> ***Proverbs 28:26 ESV "Those who trust in themselves are fools but those who walk in wisdom are kept safe."***
>
> ***Isaiah 2:22 NLT "Don't put your trust in mere humans. They are as frail as breath. What good are they?"***

More times than not, we will always go to our family, to our pastors, to our friends and or co-workers for advice; before we ever go to God and seek Him. I'm guilty! I am probably the worst about doing this. But as I have gotten older and learned the hard way of looking for advice from men. I have had to discipline myself, by going to God and seeking him first. Each day I try to practice this, but often times fumble the ball. The reason I started seeking God's advice instead of men's advice, is because to many times their advice ended up being the wrong advice.

The Bible here gives us the names of seven of his men who knew the laws. These seven men's name were:

1. Carshena- His name means, a lamb; sleeping
2. Shethar – his name means, a star.
3. Admatha- his name means, a cloud of death; a mortal vapor. Now there is a name for you. Aren't you glad you don't have this as your name.
4. Tarshish- his name means, contemplation, examination.
5. Meres- his name means, lofty.
6. Marsena- his name means, bitterness of bramble.
7. Memucan- his name means, dignified.

(from Hitchcock's Bible Name Dictionary)

This is about all we know about these men, other than they were the ones closet to him. So, he turns to them wanting to know what the Persian law says what to do with an disobedient wife? I want to interject here that some commentaries as well as from other writers said that; king Ahasuerus probably did not know how to read or write. This will be brought up again in another chapter.

Verses 16-22

"And Memucan answered before the king and the princes; "Queen Vashti has not only wronged the king, but all the princes, and all the people who are in all the provinces of King Ahasuerus.

For the queen's behavior will become known to all women, so that they will despise their husbands in their eyes, when they report, 'King Ahasuerus commanded Queen Vashti to be brought in before him, but she did not come.'

This very day the noble ladies of Persia and Media will say to all the king's officials that they have heard of the behavior of the queen. Thus there will be excessive contempt and wrath.

If it pleases the king, let a royal decree go out from him, and let it be recorded in the laws of the Persians and the Medes, so that it will not be altered, that Vashti shall come no more before King Ahasuerus; and let the king give her royal position to another who is better than she."

"When the king's decree which he will make is proclaimed throughout all his empire (for it is great), all wives will honor their husbands, both great and small."

And the reply pleased the king and the princes, and the king did according to the word of Memucan.

Then he sent letters to all the king's provinces, to each province in it's own script, and to every people in their own language, that each man should be master in his own house, and speak in the language of his own people.

According to the commentaries that I read, they all stated that there was no Persian law; on what to do with a disobedient queen, or wife. That is up until this point and time with Ahasuerus and Vashti. So what is the king do now that he has come to this point in his life and reign as king. Well, since there was no law on the books for divorce now there is going to be a law for a divorce.

Just as the king had asked this question to his trusted wise men around him. Memucan speaks up as the spokesman of the group. He tells the king that what Vashti had done, she just has not wronged you the king, but all the husbands throughout his entire kingdom. It's just like that old saying we use at times, "one bad apple ruins the entire bushel." That's all it takes isn't it!

J. Vernon McGee says in his commentary on Esther, he says something rather hilarious on this verses:

"About this time a little fellow named Memucan speaks up. He's the spokesman, and he is a henpecked husband. How do I know he's henpecked? He is afraid that, when the deed of the queen come to the attention of all women, they will look with contempt upon their husbands. Memucan is Mr. Milquetoast. If the queen gets away with this, he would not want to go home."

Now I don't know for sure if he was henpecked or not? He may have been henpecked and was afraid to go home if his wife found about this. But if it got out throughout the entire one hundred and twenty-seven provinces, there was going to be chaos for sure. So, what Memucan is suggesting is what Barney Fife tells Andy Taylor, "You've got to nip it in the bud!" "Nip it!"

So Memucan goes on to tell the king, how to remedy this situation by having a royal commandment. This royal commandment would be coming from the king himself. Once he has made this into a royal commandment, it cannot in any way be changed. This commandment is for Queen Vashti to never ever come before the king ever again. She is to be banished from the palace and for everything that she owns is to be given to another woman that is better than she is.

He goes on to say that once it is chiseled in stone, there was no turning back. Not only that, but this commandment is to be broadcast through out his entire kingdom. This way the king would be the example for all men through out his kingdom, of what happens to a disobedient wife towards her husband. For all the wives in his kingdom would then give honor to all their husbands instead of dishonor. By doing this, this would strike fear into all women in his kingdom not to act as Queen Vashti did.

God hates divorce! He created marriage between a man and a woman to be a lifetime communion between them. This is what Jesus said about divorce, in Matthew 19:4-9:

> ***"And He answered and said to them, "Have you not read that He who made them at the beginning made them at the beginning made them male and female, and said, 'For this reason a man shall leave his father and mother and be joined to his wife, and the two shall become on flesh'? So then, they ae not longer two but one flesh. Therefore, what God has joined together, let not man separate."***
>
> ***"They said to Him, "Why then did Moses command to give a certificate of divorce, and to put her away?"***
>
> ***He said to them, "Moses, because of the hardness of our hearts, permitted you to divorce your wives, but from the beginning it was not so. And I say to you, whoever divorces his wife, except for sexual immorality, and marries another, commits adultery; and whoever marries her who is divorced commits adultery."***

If a Jewish man found something wrong with his wife he could divorce her for almost any reason. If she was found out, not to be a virgin on their wedding day then he could have her stoned. But often times, if a Jewish man had married a woman, then went out and seen someone better looking than her, he could divorce her. If she didn't keep the house clean, was a bad cook and burnt supper he could divorce her for it.

But here we have a king who is a Gentile a pagan, who worshipped another god or multiple god(s). We also see that he is drunk and that they had been drinking and feasting for six months. Not only that he is beyond mad, but his anger is also a fierce anger because she didn't come to him when he asked. So in his rage of anger, he is asking them what to do. I believe that these seven men are playing off his anger, and they knew how he could be in this manner of anger bouts.

If he hadn't been in a drunken anger in front of his guest to prove to them how he settled an uprising of a disobedient wife. That he should have excused his guest, let his anger subside, then calmly went to her and talked to her, it would not have gone this far.

But notice in verse 21 what the Bible tells us. It says, "And the saying pleased the king and the princes;" The advice of Memucan please the king, it mad him happy to hear what to do with her, his anger is now happiness. But notice too that it just did not please him but the princes as well.

Then at once he had letters sent out to all the 127 provinces under his rule to let them all know what he was doing and that this was a law for all men under his rule. Now it is a law, and this law could not and would not be broken, because it's now a law of the Meds and Persians. There is no going back, what's done is done. Just like with Pilate when he wrote the subscription placed above Jesus on the cross, "King of the Jews." The Pharisees wanted him to change it to "He said, He was King of the Jews." Pilate told them, "What I have written, I have written."

Closing thoughts

To close out this first chapter, I can see here how this relates to the Lord and the nation of Israel. When we started in this chapter, we see King Ahasuerus is King over a vast kingdom, 127 provinces. We are told of his power, all his servants, his officials, and his great wealth. Then we see that he displayed his riches and splendor of his excellent majesty. And the expensive feast that he had in Shushan the citadel. Then we see how his wife Queen Vashti was disobedient to his command of coming to him.

Myself, and you may agree and disagree with me. But I believe that this relationship is a symbol of God's relationship with the nation of Israel and Judah. God is wealthy, He has a vast kingdom, He and only He is the most excellent Majesty. He sets on his throne in heaven, and it was He who had called Jacob out of Egypt. He brought Jacob out with power, signs, wonders and miracles. Then He brought Israel to Mount Sinai, and gave them the Ten Commandments, as well as the law for them to be in agreement with, and to obey only Him.

But they forsook God, worshipped other god(s), killed their children by offering them to Molech, committed adultery on God as well as their spouses, then they became perverted by committing sodomy. God sent his messengers

1: Rash Decision of a Drunk King

the Prophets for hundreds of years to get them to come back to Him, but they rebelled each time. They cheated their neighbors; they murdered one another, and the list goes on.

But here in this first chapter I see the contrast between Ahasuerus being the symbol of God and Vashti being the symbol of Israel and Judah. They had been disobedient to God for so long and they broke the marriage contract between them and God. So God put them away for 70 years.

Don't get me wrong. God loved Israel and Judah, but God hates sin. God disciplined them in His fierce anger, but He only went so far. I say that because in his fierce anger He could have annihilated them just as He did Sodom and Gomorrah, Edom and other nations He completely destroyed. So in order to discipline them He sent Babylon to do His punishing for Him, to humble them.

As I pointed out earlier. King Ahasuerus could have had Vashti killed, but he didn't, he spared her life; and gave her a bill of divorce. But as we move further on in the Book of Esther we will see that God allowed this for the saving of His people. We will see that God is always working in the life of His people to bring about His will and purpose.

J. Thomas Ruble II

2

Province Beauty Pageant

Verses 1-4

"After these things, when the wrath of King Ahasuerus subsided, her remembered Vashti, what she had done, and what had been decreed against her.

Then the king's servants who attended him said: "Let beautiful young virgins be sought for the king; and let the king appoint officers in all the provinces of his kingdom, that they may gather all the beautiful your virgins to Shushan the citadel, into the women's quarters, under the custody of Hegai the king's eunuch, custodian of the women. And let beauty preparations be given them.

Then let the young woman who pleases the king be queen instead of Vashti." This thing pleased the king, and he did so.

Here we read, "After these things." The Bible is telling us after everything that had taken place in chapter one. But history also tells us what had taken place in or around this time of 481-480 B.C. That King Ahasuerus as we know had a big party to carry out an invasion on Greece. He was defeated by Greece at Salamis and Plataea. When he returned home to the Shushan palace he had a lot on his mind, but Queen Vashti was not there to support him.

Now that he was no longer angry with Vashti, he was now missing her. This reminds me of that song in the 1980's by rock group "Cinderella, "*You Don't Know What You Got Until It's Gone.*" There is a lot of truth to those words. Believe me, because I had to spend a weekend one time without my wife while she helped our ailing dad. Dad had become a suspect of having Covid 19 and spent eight weeks in hospital and nursing home recovering. All of us kids took turns staying with him or helping him do things around the house or get groceries for him.

So, while I had to work at the factory all weekend on my shift, my wife stayed him to help him out. I was miserable! It felt like you chopped off my right arm, left leg and shot my dog. She missed me just as much as I missed her. We called and text each other more during that weekend than we did the years we've had cell phones. I took the pillow she left and hugged it until I squeezed all the feathers out of it. Lonely!

That's what is happing to King Ahasuerus here. He is missing her by rewinding his mental tape recorder and playing it over and over. Now there was no going back to her and saying, "I'm sorry for getting angry, please come back home." Nope, can't do that now because that bridge has been burnt down.

All the men who served the king had noticed how moody and lonely the king was. He was a different man now that Vashti wasn't around and he was not throwing a party. Instead of being his happy go lucky drunken self, he had become a Gloomy Gus. So, they needed to do something to cheer the king up and to get his mind off of Vashti not being around.

So, they come up with a plan of finding beautiful young virgins to be brought to the king. What better way to cheer the king up, we know that he loves the women, and this will get his mind off Vashti. In order to carry out this plan, the king would appoint officers in all the provinces of his kingdom; to find them and bring them to him in the palace in Shushan.

We are never told just how many young virgins there were? Nor are we told just how old these virgins were? There could have been as many as five hundred to twelve hundred virgins that was brought to Shushan. And I am guessing that they were at least fourteen years old to seventeen years old. Most of the material I read said that they were fourteen years old. This sounds accurate because during these days that is when a young woman to typically married.

Once they arrived to the palace they would be kept in the house of women. This probably is the house were the kings harem was kept. The man in charge of this house of women would have been Hege or Hegai. His name means- meditation, word, grooming separation. He was a eunuch which means he was a man who had been castrated, one employed to guard women's living areas at an oriental court. From Got Questions.com gives this description of why

2: Province Beauty Pageant

king's made men eunuchs. A king would have his slaves castrated to ensure a king's advisers did not have children or romantic interests that might tempt them towards betrayal. This procedure was intended to make the subject asexual, disinterested in sex, lacking sexual urges and unable to produce children. So this is about all we know about Hegai, other than he was a eunuch and that he was in charge of the house of women. I want to know how he managed to stay sane, with all those hens in the hen house. Can you image all the talking, giggling, whining and complaining.

The one thing that I know is that man is a very consentient being! Because one thing men love is beautiful women. Believe me I know, because when I was younger that what I wanted was a beautiful wife one day. I seen it when I was in the Army, especially the day the Dallas Cowboy Cheerleaders came with the USO to put on a show. Even our Chaplin was at the show drooling, with his eyes popping out of his head.

Now this very well could be Memucan who is giving the king this advice of having a beauty contest. Because after all he was the one who gave the king the advice of giving Vashti a divorce. His advice this time was for beautiful young virgins to be brought about before the king in choosing a new queen for the kingdom. And this man's advice was once again pleasing to the king. Why? Because one he would be the judge of this contest, and he would be viewing all these young women. Oh yeah! What better way to find a wife right.

I remember an episode of Andy Griffith where a man named Jeff Pruitt came to town looking for a wife. So, he was standing on the corner of a street, watching the women walk by. As they walked by, he would pick them up into the air and smile. While he was in the process of doing this, Andy and Barney noticed what he was doing. Jeff Pruitt was being smart or smooth about finding himself a wife. If you did this today, you'd get slapped by the woman or arrested by a cop.

Let me interject here by saying this, "Outer beauty isn't everything to women." Some of you like me have meet some very beautiful women in our lifetime. But under that thin layer of beauty, there is a beast inside some of them. Now that goes for us men to, we can also be a beast as well. But we men always place so much importance on the outward beauty of the women.

I think I know why we do this to an extent! First of all it is because by nature we are sinful creatures. Second, I believe its from the stories read to us about beauty and living happily ever after. Last, because of how Hollywood depicts true love in the movies.

In Proverbs 31:30, God's word tells us this about beauty.

"Charm is deceptive, and beauty does not last; but a woman who fears the LORD is to be praised."

Beauty does not last! The writer here is absolutely right that it doesn't last. The reason it doesn't last is because of sin and the process of aging. Sometime when you have time, look back at pictures of you and your family when we were younger. We had thick hair, nice smooth skin, no wrinkles, no grey hair, or bags under our eyes. After doing this look at a picture of us today or them today, comparing younger to older. Are we as good looking and beautiful as we were when we were younger. No we are not, we look like a bad Paper Mache project.

More less this beauty contest is satisfy, gratify, the lust of the king. Just like with these beauty contest held for Ms. America as well as other beauty contest. It is just for men to set around drink and lust after women. This isn't any way to find out about the person's character at all.

If you're looking for a girlfriend, boyfriend, husband or wife based off they're outward appearance, be careful. Because sometimes, often times the wrapping of the package can be misleading of what's really inside that person.

Introduction of Mordecai

Verses 5-7

"In Shushan the citadel there was a certain Jew whose name was Mordecai the son of Jair, the son of Shimei, the son of Kish, a Benjamite."

"Kish had been carried away from Jerusalem with the captives who had been captured with Jeconiah king of Judah, whom Nebuchadnezzar the king of Babylon had carried away."

"And Mordecai had brought up Hadassah that is Esther, his uncle's daughter, for she had neither father nor mother. The

young woman was lovely and beautiful. When her father and mother died, Mordecai took her as his own daughter."

Here in verse five we see that the story has taken a different direction now. Up to this point everything has been about a Gentile king, his palace, his court, his servants, drinking, partying, his campaigning and throwing around his money. It's also been about his beautiful Queen Vashti, her disobedience to him, him giving her a divorce, and the beginning of a beauty pageant.

But here in this verse we are introduced to a Jewish man named Mordecai. This man was living in the citadel of Shushan. So what do we know about this man? According to Smith's Bible Dictionary, he describes him as follows:

"We read here that his fathers name was Jair. His name means- (enlightener). His Grandfather's name was Shimei. His name means (renowned). He was from the tribe of Benjamin, before the 479 B.C. Then there was Kish, his name means- (a bow). He was the father of Shimei, and he was Mordecai's great grandfather."

So we have four generations of men here. But the question is, why would a Jewish man be living in a palace of Gentiles?

It all goes back to the time when Babylon went into the land of Judah, into the city of Jerusalem and defeated them. Which a lot of the commentaries I read said that Mordecai was taken captive at a very young age, in 597 B.C. This would have been the second wave of Nebuchadnezzar had taken captives from Jerusalem to Babylon.

I myself believe, from the way I read it, is this is a genealogy. This genealogy begins with Mordecai and takes us back to his grandfather Kish. There is a break from verse five to verse six, which says, "the son of Kish, a Benjamite who had been carried away from Jerusalem with the captivity. So I believe that it was Kish and possibly his son Shimei who was carried away to Babylon; and that Mordecai was not with them when taken to Babylon. Which means that Mordecai and possibly his father were born in captivity. We must remember that they were there for seventy years. Read Jeremiah 29:4-7.

We can trace this back that it was Kish who was taken, because it was during the time when Jeconiah, or better known as Jehoiachin. He reigned for only three months and ten days.

2 Chronicles 36:9 *"Jehoiachin was eighteen years old when he became king and he reigned three months and ten days in Jerusalem. He did what was evil in the sight of the Lord."*

But now we see that Mordecai is in Persia, in Shushan the citadel, the king's palace. The reason for him being in Persia, was because near the end of the Jews seventy years in Babylon, Cyrus the Great took the city. Upon doing so the Jews were granted freedom to return to their homeland of Israel. But some had decided to stay in Persia and live there instead of returning to Israel.

Let me point out that those who returned to their native land were in the will of God. Those who remained were out of the will of God. So we see that Mordecai was out of the will of God. But just because we get out of the will of God does not mean that He does not love us, or give up on us. However, He will bring about and allow things to happen in our lives to bring us back into His will. With some of us it takes a little longer than some to get the message. I'm speaking about myself here, not the one reading this. That is up to you to determine if you are or not in the will of God?

Mordecai we see was a very loving, compassionate and carrying man. We see from verse seven that he took his cousin Hadassah or better known as Esther to be his daughter. The Bible is silent on the names of her parents, nor does it tell us how or when they died? But we see that Mordecai took Esther in to be his daughter and to raise her.

If you recall, Abraham also did this when his brother Haran died and took his son lot with him to the land of Canaan. Lot stayed with his uncle for quite some time, before departing from him after a quarrel with their herdsmen took place.

In our world today, we notice that there are a lot of grandparents who are now raising their grandchildren. The reason for this happening is due to numerous reasons, but the main reason is due to addictions. But one of the biggest reasons is because this generation is just lazy and irresponsible.

But notice that here in the verse seven the writer calls her by two names. Her Hebrew name is Hadassah, which means- (myrtle). Then her Persian name is Esther, which means- (Star). Myself I like that name Hadassah, it is a very beautiful name I think.

Then notice that it says that she was a young woman. The old King James Version calls her a maid. When they use this name for a young woman, it doesn't mean that she was young woman who worked for someone around the house. A maid or Maiden means- was a young girl, a virgin, and unmarried. If you recall in the New Testament in the Book of Luke, Luke 1:38 Mary called herself a maidservant of the Lord. As I stated earlier, she could have been any where from fourteen to seventeen. There was a few sites on line that I looked up, that said Esther was around 50- 70 years old. I knew that couldn't be right because the Bible says that she was a young woman.

Not only was she his adopted daughter, but that she was lovely and beautiful. The King James Version says that she was fair and beautiful. Both these words mean the same thing, so it is telling us that she was extremely beautiful. In today's terms, she was a knockout!

I remember a joke that I heard several years ago about Adam talking to God about how beautiful Eve was.

Adam: "God. Why did you make Eve so beautiful and attractive?"

God: "So you would love her!"

Adam: "Why did you make her so soft?"

God: "So you would love her!"

Adam: "Why did you make her so dumb?"

God: "So she'd love you?"

There you have it. We love women for their beauty, but it takes someone special to love someone like us.

Let's not forget this. God's name is never mentioned in this book at all, but we can see that He is at work. Because later on in this chapter we will see how God is working in the life of this man and his adopted daughter Esther. God always, always sees the beginning from the end, but we do not have that capability. I don't believe that He believes in beauty contest, but He can intervene and turn it the way He wants it to be.

Verses 8-11

So it was, when the king's command and decree were heard, and when many young women were gathered at Shushan the citadel, under the custody of Hegai, that Esther also was taken to the king's palace, into the care of Heagi the custodian of the women.

Now the young woman pleased him, and she obtained his favor; so he readily gave beauty preparations to her, besides her allowance. Then seven choice maidservants were provided for her from the king's palace, and he moved her and her maidservants to the best place in the house of the women.

Esther had not revealed her people or family, for Mordecai had charged her not to reveal it.

And every day Mordecai paced in front of the court of the women's quarters, to learn of Esther's welfare and what was happening to her.

The king's command was made into law throughout his kingdom and was carried out. There were woman coming into the palace from all over the kingdom. The Bible just says many, so we don't have an accurate number of how many young women there was.

When they arrived at the palace, they were all placed into the care of Hegai. This is the same man in verse three of chapter two. In this verse we just have a different way of spelling his name.

Then we see Esther being brought in with all these other young women. So she is now brought to Hegai and into the king's house. But notice at what verse nine here says, "and the maiden pleased him and she obtained favor of him." This is telling us that God has broken in on the scene now. How do we know this? Well let's look at some more scriptures of other Bible Characters.

Let's start first with Joseph, the son of Jacob and Rachel. Remember Joseph was mistreated by his brothers, because he was their father's favorite. He had made him a coat of many colors and they hated him because of it. But they hated him even more because of the dreams that he had and told to them.

One day Jacob sent Joseph to his brothers to see how they were doing. So he went looking for them and they noticed him coming towards them. Next thing Joseph knew, they tore his coat of many colors off him, and wanted to kill him. But the oldest brother Reuben, talked them out of killing him and placing him into a pit. He did this in order to come back and rescue him later, but that didn't happen. Reuben wasn't there, so the other brothers took and sold him to the caravan of Ishmaelite's for twenty pieces of silver. Upon his arrival to Egypt, he was sold again to Potiphar. This is what the Bible tells us in Genesis 39:4 NKJV:

> ***"So Joseph found favor in his sight and served him. Then he made him overseer of his house and all that he had he put under his authority."***

Next, there was Noah! Genesis 6:8 ESV "Noah found favor in the eyes of the Lord." Then there was Daniel, in Daniel 1:9 ESV "And God gave Daniel favor and compassion in the sight of the chief of eunuchs." Then we see that the Lord had this favor on Him in Luke 2:52, "And Jesus increased in wisdom and in stature and in favor with God and man."

What this means is – finding favor means gaining approval, acceptance or special benefits or blessings. There is also a close association among favor, with grace, and mercy, which is used to translate the same Hebrew and Greek words such as hen (ej) and charis (cavri). The favor that human beings receive from God depends on his good pleasure and is often extended into response to prayer and righteous living. (From Baker's Evangelical Dictionary of Biblical Theology.)

I believe that when Hegai seen Esther he seen something deeper than her outward beauty. I believe when he seen her that he knew deep down inside himself, "this is the next queen." I believe that this favor was of God Himself shining through Esther. She carried herself in a moral and respective manner. She wasn't flirty, suggestive, and making eyes. Only God can provide this type of favor among those who are enemies or different in culture areas.

We also know that God has shown up by what the rest of the verse tells us.

> ***"and he speedily gave her things for purification, with such things as belonged to her,"***

She was given the things that she needed to make her more beautiful and healthier. This would have been food and oils that they used in those days and times. So Hegai wasn't wasting any time here, so he sped up the process with Esther. He gave her seven maids to her from the king's house, which would have been teaching her the ways and customs of the queen in the palace. And last of all she was given the best room in the house. All of this is the best, and only the best comes from God Himself.

Here in verse ten, we see that Mordecai had told Esther before going into the palace. That it would be wise not to mention that she was a Hebrew from the land of Judah and Jerusalem. With him telling her to remain quite about this, was the same as denying her identity to God, and the religion of her people. So we see here that Esther is obedient to Mordecai, by not mentioning her nationality.

Have we ever done this to God, in order to be cool or part of the crowd? Do we know anyone who has ever done this? What I'm talking about it is this. Have there been times in our Christian walk with Christ, that we never mentioned it to those around us. For instance, at school, at work, at a gathering outside of the church building. The last thing we want people to know is that we're Christians, we go to church, and how we stand on the Word of God and what He says about sin. Jesus warns against this in Luke 9:26 NKJV:

"For whoever is ashamed of Me and My words, of him the Son of Man will be ashamed when He comes in His own glory, and in His Father's, and of the Holy Angels."

Yes! Being a Jew or identifying oneself as a Jew in this day and time would have been very dire. We know this because Nebuchadnezzar hated the Jews, as well as the other surrounding nations around them. They hated them now and they hate them to this very day. We know this by reading the Book of Daniel. Daniel and his three friends Shadrach, Meshach and Abednego, were looked down upon and mistreated during Nebuchadnezzar's reign.

His three friends were criticized and persecuted for not bowing down to the image created by Nebuchadnezzar. When they wouldn't compromise, they were thrown into the fiery furnace. But they survived because the Lord walked through the fire with them. Why? Because they stood up for God and their convictions. God's first commandment was that they should have no other gods before Him.

They didn't stop there with their ways of trying to get rid of Daniel either. They forced King Darius to make a law of the Meds and Persians, that anyone praying to a different god other than himself or one of their gods. That the person that was caught doing this was to be thrown into the lion's den. The reason they did this was because of their jealousy towards Daniel and the king promoting him. And also, they did it because they knew his daily habits of praying three times to God everyday. So King Darius singed this into a law. The next thing we see that they found him out and they threw him into the lion's den.

However, King Darius couldn't sleep that night and the next morning he went to the lion's den to check on Daniel. Upon his arrival he yelled in there to see if Daniel was still alive. When he found out that the lions had not torn him apart, because God had shut their mouths. He had Daniel brought out of the lion's den then they threw the men who had plotted against Daniel.

1 Peter 3:15 "But sanctify the Lord God in your hearts, and always be ready to give a defense to everyone who asks you a reason for the hope that is in you, with meekness and fear."

Yes, it is hard to be a Christian, very hard, especially in the world we live in today. We either shrink from being known as a Christian, or we stand up to the world to be known as a Christian.

I remember a time in my Christian walk to where, I had been put on the spot one day at work. I hadn't told very many people there that I was a Christian. Mostly it was due to how our dad raised us. He always said to let our actions as a Christian to speak for us, unless people ask you why your different and don't believe like they do.

There were several of us working on products at this table. Most of the young men and women there was telling dirty jokes, cursing, and talking about sex. This one young man was the worst of all, and he was always saying dirty things to his girlfriend.

On this one particular day, she all at once pointed me out to her boyfriend saying, "Why can't you be more like him?" He started using foul language and got really mad at her and me. Then all at once his girlfriend ask me, "Why are you different? How come you don't talk like everyone else at the table?" That's when I told all of them that I was a Christian, and that Jesus had changed me.

After I made that statement, you could have heard a pin drop. Everyone at the table was embarrassed for how they had been talking in front of me. From that time on until some of them left that place, they were careful in how they talked and what they talked about. If I remember correctly that girl that asked me that questioned end up going to church, accepting Jesus as Lord and Savior and left that young man she had been dating.

With all that being said. We come now to verse eleven and we see that Mordecai is just like a long tail cat in a room of rocking chairs.

Let's not forget that first of all Mordecai was Esther's legal guardian. Then we seen earlier that he was also a worker in the king's palace. So with him being in this place would not have aroused any supposition of his presence there. Everyone there knew him or had recognized him from working there.

Here I believe that he is showing parental love and care for Esther. He was just like all of us who have children or grandchildren. When they are gone somewhere and they are out of our reach of protection, we're going to wonder what is going on with them. So he comes by that way every day where Esther was staying to find out what was going on with her. I can imagine that he was wondering if they found out if she was Jewish? What if they don't like her? What's going on with my daughter? Why did I ever put her in this predicament? Well let's move on with our story to see what happens next.

Verses 12-14

"Each young woman's turn came to go in to King Ahasuerus after she had completed twelve months' preparation, according to the regulations for the women, for thus were the days of their preparation apportioned: six months with oil of myrrh, and six months with perfumes and preparations for beautifying women."

"Thus prepared, each young woman went to the king, and she was given whatever she desired to take with her from the women's quarters to the king's palace."

"In the evening she went, and in the morning she returned to the second house of the women, to the custody of Shaashgaz, the king's eunuch who kept the concubines. She would not go in to the king again unless the king delighted in her and called for her by name."

I remember as a boy growing up how almost all the women in our community would go to the beauty parlor. They would go there to get their hair washed, cut, dyed, or to get a perm. I also remember how this frustrated our grandfather when our grandmother would go to the beauty parlor. We kids would ask him "where she was going"? He would say jokingly, "Aw! She's going to her skull fixed!" We knew what he meant that she was going to the beauty parlor.

Often when they went, they were gone for an hour or two. But here in this verse we see that these women spent a whole year at the beauty parlor; before going in to see the king. Can you imagine the price tag on a whole year at the beauty parlor?

Now don't get me wrong! I believe that women should take a little pride in how they look, but some women take it way to far. Think about it men! If our wives didn't shower, fix their hair nice, dress in nice clothes or deodorant, we would not have gone out with them. Nobody would want to go out with someone who hasn't showered in four weeks, brushed their hair and teeth for the same amount of time. The smell would have been putrid.

But in today's society men and women both spend thousands of dollars every year to look good on the outside. Women will spend a lot of money on cosmetics, hairdo's, getting nails done, sun tanning, costly soaps, shampoo's, perfume, jewelry, and wardrobe.

I believe one of the reason's is because of vanity. The next reason why is because of Hollywood setting a high standard on outward appearance. But once you take off all that makeup off them, their outward beauty disappears. I'm a very blessed man to have a wife that doesn't wear all of that and spends lots of money on all that beauty aids. She didn't even wear it on our wedding day, and to me she was the most beautiful woman in the world; and still is to this day.

Aren't you glad that God does not accept any of us on our outward appearance. If He did everyone who ever lived is in serious trouble. In 1 Samuel 16:7 KJV, God said this about David to Samuel:

> **"But the Lord said to Samuel, look not on his countenance, or on the height of his stature; because I have refused him. For the Lord sees not as man sees; for man look's, on the outward appearance but the Lord looks at the heart."**

If we looked at people the way God does, there would be less confusion in the church, as well as the world today. If people today put as much effort into having a personal relationship with Jesus as they do with fixing up our outward appearance. You see God's idea of a King of Israel was different than Samuel's idea of a king.

Samuel was thinking on terms as man today, of what a leader should look like. He should be tall, handsome, the awards on his wall, his or her academic achievement's. But God was looking at the heart of David, and God even told him that David was a man after God's on heart. Now why would He say this? God is compassionate, merciful, kind, good, and rules with wisdom. The same held true for David, he cared about the things of God and doing it right.

In 1 Peter 3:3 the Word of God tells us this:

"Don't be concerned about the outward beauty of fancy hairstyles, expensive jewelry or beautiful clothes."

The real you isn't the outward appearance of you, the real you is inside. Jesus Christ paid for your soul with His life blood on the cross. He died so that you would have life eternally. Sure, He wants you to take care of our bodies, but more importantly He wants us to take care of the soul part, because that is the most important of all. Because to die without His is to live eternally separated from Him in hell, for all eternity. All of our good looks, and good works will not get us into heaven.

Last of all, all of us have to face reality that our bodies are going to grow old. With each passing year, we are going to lose our hair, get grey hair, go bald, get wrinkles, have aches and pains, get sagging skin. It's all because of sin, and the effect sin has had on our bodies as well as the world itself.

But each young woman came before the king, as they had come in line, and having a full year of beauty treatments. Each one of them was given liberty to choose the things they wanted before going in before the king. These women wanted to look their very best for him, in order to be chosen queen.

They would spend the evening with him in his house and then leave in the morning time. After doing so they returned to the second house of women. This is the place where these young women did not want to find themselves. Because this second house of women was where they kept the king's concubines. They were not the wife or wives of the king, they were his mistresses. The only time he would see them was when he called for them by name or when he desired them.

This was not what God intended from the beginning. The reason they had a harem was because of the lust of the flesh. No one else could have her so they would take and lock them away.

Notice that one of the ingredients use in the beauty aid was myrrh. This oil was quoted 156 times in the Scriptures. It was using as an holy anointing oil, as an ointment, an incense, a embalming ingredient and here as a skin beauty treatment. (from Dr. Axe.com.) This ointment was one of the gifts that the wise men brought to Jesus, when He was around two years of age.

Once they were brought to the house of women, Hegai was no longer in charge of them. Another eunuch by the name of Shaashgaz, was in charge of the concubines. This is the reason why Mordecai was pacing back and forth and visiting to see what had become of Esther. This would not have been a good thing to happen to a young Jewish woman. This would have brought about shame on her as well as her family.

Verses 15-18

"Now when the turn came for Esther the daughter of Abihail the uncle of Mordecai, who had taken her as his daughter, to go in to the king, she requested nothing but what Hegai the king's eunuch, the custodian of the women, advised. And Esther obtained favor in the sight of all who saw her."

"So Esther was taken to King Ahasuerus, into his royal palace, in the tenth month, which is the month of Tebeth, in the seventh year of his reign."

"The king loved Esther more than all the other women, and she obtained grace and favor in this sight more than all the virgins; so he set the royal crown upon her head and made her queen instead of Vashti."

"Then the king made a great feast, the Feast of Esther, for all his officials and servants; and he proclaimed a holiday in the provinces and gave gifts according to the generosity of the king."

Esther was next young woman in line to go into the king's room to be judged by him. I would say that she is a little nervous, because after all, all the other young women had been sent to the second house of the king. All of us can sympathize with this young woman. How many times have we had the butterflies in our stomach when we had to sing, preach, or teach, or anything to that matter. I have been so nervous before singing, preaching or giving a testimony that I became ill. So, I had to pray and ask the Lord for his help.

But then notice that the writer here mentions Esther's real father Abihail, and her cousin who had adopted her. The writer is making it known of her family linage. It is also telling us that Mordecai was the one who had taken her to be his daughter. I can imagine that after all his worrying and pacing, he was very proud of his adopted daughter.

Then we see that Esther did not request anything for herself, except for what Hegai the eunuch advised her to take or use. She was placing herself wholeheartedly into this man's hands to come through this the winner. I believe these two gained a lot of trust with each other over the year together.

Remember back in verse 9, that Esther had pleased Hegai, and had found favor in his eyes. She not only had found favor in his eyes, but to all those who seen her coming. Just like a bride on her wedding day, when the music starts, everyone turns to see her coming. Everyone is so captivated by her radiant beauty, there is a hush over the crowd; then everyone smiles and comments on her and her beautiful white dress.

This favor that is upon her here isn't anything she has done, or Hegai has done, or the beauty treatments have done. All of this was being done because of what God was doing. This favor is the very grace, peace, and mercy of God. His favor, being done watching from the shadows.

The writer is very in depth, of the time that this took place with Esther going into his room. When this took place it was the tenth month which is the month Tebeth. The name Tebeth is the tenth month on the Jewish calendar and the fourth month of the secular calendar. It ran from mid-December to mid-January. (from JW.org)

Also notice here that four years now has passed from the time of his divorce from Vashti. Because in chapter one verse three we see that he was in his third year of reign as king. It may have been four years since the divorce but now he has found the one to take Vashti's place. The Bible tells us her in verse seventeen that the king loved her more than all the women. Not only did he love her but she found grace and favor in the eyes of the king.

God is working here in the life of this young woman as well as in the life of the nation of Israel. This is the power of God working. First she found favor with Hegai, then she found favor with all of those who looked upon her, now she has found favor and grace with the king.

The word Grace means- unmerited divine assistance given to humans for their regeneration or sanctification. A virtue coming from God. Approval. This is the same way that Christ views the Church, is with Grace and favor. This grace was a virtue coming from God Himself. Esther had found favor and the approval of the king. I believe when King Ahasuerus looked at her there wasn't lust in his eyes. I believe he seen something in her, that all the other young woman didn't have.

From these verses here I can see a symbolic picture of Israel here, showing us the unmerited Grace of God towards Israel and the church. First, I see that although Israel had sinned against God, and how He disciplined them Spiritually, through seventy years of captivity. God did not wipe them out completely, when He could have done so, by using Babylon. However, Israel found grace and favor in the sight of God, just as Esther had found favor and grace with the king. He left a remnant of Israel to return to their homeland. This is telling us that although they had sinned against Him, He still wasn't finished with them. We know this because He promised that the Messiah would be born through Abraham and his seed. We know this to be true by what the Bible tells us in the Gospels of Matthew and Luke.

Next I can see how this relates to the Church, the Bride of Christ.

> ***2 Timothy 1:9 "He has saved us and called us to a holy life- not because of anything we have done but because of his own purpose and grace. This grace was given us in Christ Jesus before the beginning of time."***

All true believer's who make up the Bride of Christ is the church. None of us did any thing of ourselves to earn the grace of God. This was on God's behalf of loving us and granting us grace and favor before Him; for what His Son did on the cross. This grace was granted to us even before God created the world. Amazing Grace, how sweet the sound, that saved a wretch like me,

I once was lost but no I am found was blind but now I see. Thank you Father, for your Amazing Grace, thank You for Your Son Jesus who died for us while we were wretched, wicked and sinful.

One last thought. Esther is not here by luck, chance or coincidence. No! She is here because of God in all of His infinite glory and wisdom. Before He created the world, He had planned this moment in the future. Now His plan was being fulfilled in her, just as His plan for the coming of His Son born of a virgin would one day be fulfilled. His plan of His Son dying a sacrificial death on the cross, being buried and arising again on the third day. God is still in control of everything in the universe and in the world as we know it.

When we began this story of Esther in chapter one, it began with the king having a feast. You would think that King Ahasuerus was an American as much as he likes to drink and party. He reminds me of that T.G. Sheppard song *"Party Time."* It appears that this king likes to party, eat, drink and be merry. But this feast was for Queen Esther and upon her becoming the new queen. All the royal people as well as his servants were at this feast, thrown in her honor as the new queen.

A Jewish wedding is called a Seudat. In Hebrew this word Seudat means "wedding feast or marriage supper." This is a great reminder to us of the Great Marriage Supper of the Lamb. This marriage supper is for the Bride of Christ, His Church. Jesus placed great importance on marriage.

In John 2:1-12, we see that Jesus and his disciples were invited to a wedding in Cana. This is where we see his very first miracle of turning water into wine. In Matthew 19 we see that Jesus places importance of marriage. The Pharisees were trying to trap Him about a man divorcing his wife, but Jesus turned it on them by saying this about marriage.

> ***Matthew 19:4-6 "Haven't you read the scriptures? Jesus replied. They record that from the beginning God made them male and female. And He said, This explains why a man leaves his father and mother and is joined to his wife and the two are united into one. Since they are no longer two but one let no one split apart what God has joined together."***

The only time that God said that something was not good during creation; was when He said that it is not good for man to be alone. So God placed Adam into a deep sleep, performed the first operation by taking out his rib. From this rib He made a woman and brought the woman to Adam.

God created them male and female, so God is the One who created marriage; and for marriage to be between a man and woman. He created it to be beautiful, but today man has turned it into a bed of defilement.

Just as he made a feast for his newly crowned queen, he also brought about relief of all the provinces paying taxes for a year. Some of the commentaries I read, said that it also released men from military duty and serving in jail.

One day Jesus Christ is going to have a great feast with His Bride the Church. There will be no more sin, no more war, famines and no more death. This will be a time of rejoicing and celebrating, peace with the Lamb for all eternity. What a glorious day that will be, to sit around the table with Jesus and eat a supper prepared by Him.

Verses 19-23

"When the virgins were gathered together a second time, Mordecai sat within the king's gate."

"Now Esther had not revealed her family and her people, just as Mordecai had charged her, for Esther obeyed the command of Mordecai as when she was brought up by him."

"In those days, while Mordecai sat within the king's gate two of the king's eunuchs, Bigthan and Teresh doorkeepers, became furious and sought to lay hands on King Ahasuerus."

"So the matter became known to Mordecai, who told Queen Esther, and Esther informed the king in Mordecai's name."

"And when an inquiry was made into the matter, it was confirmed, and both were hanged on a gallows; and it was written in the book of the chronicles in the presence of the king."

Some of the commentaries I read did not go into details about the first part of verse nineteen. But it left me scratching my head as why would there be a second gathering together of the virgins? But as I read verses 18-19 together,

I believe a second viewing was done in order to have a runner up, just in case things went with Esther as they had with Vashti.

The rest of verse 19 tells us, "then Mordecai sat in the king's gate." This is telling that Mordecai was setting at his job, he himself was a servant to the king. Now he was settled in his spirit, knowing that Esther has been crowned queen. But this part of the verse is a prelude to the rest of the chapter.

Verse 20 tells us once again that Esther had not made it known that she was a Jewish woman nor made it known of her people there in the citadel. But we can see what an obedient young woman she is, by listening to Mordecai. She still had not told anyone that she was Jewish, that Mordecai was her guardian. She was obedient to him as a child, as a young woman and even while a newly crowned queen. This tells us a lot about Esther and that she is a very good young woman.

This tells us a lot about Mordecai as well and what a good parent he was bring her up in the law of Moses. I believe that the two of them had very good relationship with God as well with one another. After all respect and honor begins in the relationship with family.

The Bible tells us in Proverbs 22:6 *"Train up a child in the way he should go and when he is old, he will not depart from it."*

There is a lot of truth to that verse. If you raise up a child in the Word of the Lord, praying, studying God's Word and going to church; they'll stay with it. Sometimes that will get a little sidetracked from the Lord, but the Lord has His ways of bringing them back.

We see that Esther has everything she needs to be a good queen. She has a humble spirit, she has wisdom, she has respect for those above her. She is pure from the inside to the outside. She is a very virtuous woman, as described in Proverbs 31.

To finish up this chapter, in verses 21-23, we see what began back in verse 19. We also see at the beginning of verse 22 that this was written in past tense. Because it starts out in those days, that means at the present time while Mordecai was a gate keeper.

While he was attending the king's gate, he overheard two eunuchs Bigthan and Teresh, who were guards at the door where the king slept. They were to be the most trusted people to the king, but ended up being his worst enemies. We too should be very cautious of those who are closes to us. The Bible warns us against this in Micah 7:5 NLT, ***"Don't trust anyone- not your best friend or even your wife!"*** The only one we should really trust is the Lord Himself, Proverbs 3:5-6; Proverbs 18:24.

The Bible is silent for the reason these two men were angry with the king and wanted to kill him. Not going to speculate, why they were angry with him, they were angry, and angry enough to kill him. So when they thought that the coast was clear and no one was around to hear them. They made plans in how to kill him. One small oversight on their part, they were not alone at all. And once again this was not by happenstance; Mordecai was in the right place, right time, God's appointed time.

Once Mordecai heard of their plan, he wasted no time in telling it to Queen Esther about the plot. When Esther found out about the plot she told the king about it. When he heard what Queen Esther told him, he had an investigation done to find out if it was true or not. When he had concrete evidence that the plot against his life was true, he had them hanged on a tree. Some say that they were impaled which means they were placed on a very sharp steak.

It's ironic as well as sad, to know that times have changed since then. Back in these days they believed in capital punishment, unlike people today in our society. Once something was found out back in these days they punished the person for the crime(s) they committed. Today, people go to extremes to save someone who have killed one person or many people. Then they will stand up for a woman to murder a child that is in her womb. A baby that is helpless and defenseless has no chance at all, but person who murderers someone in cold blood will be defended.

For the past thirty to fifty years, they have been slapping people on the hand and turn them loose. When they are freed of the crime, they will go out kill again and commit a more egregious crime against humanity. Friends, make no mistake about it! They may get away with it now, but there is coming a day when they will not have a leg to stand on before Almighty God.

In closing: Mordecai made it known about this plot on the king's life and it was found to be true. However, he was not awarded for making it known even though Esther had told this information in Mordecai's name. He may not have been rewarded right then and there, and that may seem unfair. But we are not always rewarded for doing the right thing at that very moment.

This action of Mordecai's was written down in the Chronicles of Persian King. The same holds true for us today, doing the work of God. Sometimes he awards us right then and there, but often times He reserves to hold this for another special time. Don't forget! God is working here. This has His handy work written all over it.

If you feel like that you've been overlooked and awarded for something, you did that was right. God has reserved that for a special time and place. It may be next month, next year, ten years or twenty years from now. But just because He withholds it for now isn't because he is unfair. His ways are different than our ways, His thoughts different than our thoughts. Pay day is coming, and what a pay day it will be, Amen! Amen!

3

"Promotion of a Wicked Man"

Verse 1

"After these things did King Ahasuerus promote Haman the son of Hammedatha the Agaite and advanced him, and set his seat above all the prince that were with him."

Here again the writer of the Book of Esther starts out as they did in the chapter two of verse one. "After these things." The things they are speaking of is the beauty contest that lasted for a year. 2) Esther being chosen as the next queen of the kingdom. 3) The feast that was given to Esther for becoming queen. 4) How Mordecai had spoiled a plot to kill the king.

Also, the writer is telling us that something else was taking place, after all the things that had taken place in chapter two. It is telling us about the king promoting a man named Haman, whose father was Hammedatha who was an Agagite. The name Haman means- noise or tumult. His fathers name means- He that troubles the law. There is not known of his father except being known as the Agagite.

The first time we learn of the Amalekites is in Exodus Chapter 17:8-16. The Amalekites came down to attack the Children of Israel. Moses told Joshua to choose some of their men to go out and fight against Amalek. So Joshua did as Moses had commanded him to do. But while Joshua and his men were going to be in battle, Moses, Aaron and Hur would be on top of a hill.

Moses held up his hands in the air, and as he did the children of Israel would prevail against the Amalekites. But when his arms grew tired the Amalekites would prevail against Israel. So Aaron and Hur moved a stone for Moses to sit on and then Aaron held up one arm while Hur held up the other arm. So Joshua and the Israel Army had a victory against them.

The Lord told Moses to write this for a memorial in a book, and to rehearse it in the ears of Joshua. Because God said that He would utterly put out the remembrance of Amalek from under heaven.

Moses built an altar there and called the name of it Jehovahnissi: Because the Lord had sworn that the Lord will have war with Amalek from generation to generation.

We are introduced to the Amalekites again, in 1 Samuel 15, when God told Samuel to tell King Saul to attach them and to completely destroy these people. The reason God told King Saul to do this is because Amalek ambushed Israel when they had come out of Egypt.

Sadly, King Saul did not do as the Lord had told him to do. He did not destroy all the people and all the herds they had. In fact, King Saul allowed Agag to live. The name Agag was not a formal name, it was a title for the king just like Pharaoh was in Egypt and Abimelech for the Philistines. (Definition from Got Questions.com)

So, King Ahasuerus made Haman, the Prime Minister of his kingdom. He was second in command to King Ahasuerus. This was the same title that Joseph had been promoted to in Egypt. The only one who had more power than him was the king. So out of all his servants he promotes this man to this position above all his servants.

Verses 2-4

"And all the king's servants who were within the king's gate bowed and paid homage to Haman, for so the king had commanded concerning him. But Mordecai would not bow or pay homage."

"Then the king's servants who were within the king's gate said to Mordecai, "Why do you transgress the king's command?"

"Now it happened, when they spoke to him daily and he would not listen to them, that they told it to Haman, to see whether Mordecai's words would stand; for Mordecai had told them that he was a Jew."

All the servants who were at the king's gate bowed down and paid homage to Haman. This homage was a special honor or respect shown publicly for a feudal allegiance. All of his servants would have been his bodyguards, judges, gate keepers and so on. Although Mordecai was one of these, because he was at this gate. But he would not bow to Haman and give him the respect due to him.

Before moving on allow me to explain to you what is meant by the king's gate here. According to Crossroads Bible Church, Kris Udd explains it.

"Although excavations have been carried out at Susa since mid 1880s, archaeologist only discovered the king's gate in 1970. It is located about 260 feet to the east of the palace. The gate was set at the edge of the moat that separated the palace complex from the royal city. A bridge across the moat ended at this gate, thus ensuring that it controlled access to the entire palace complex."

"This gate was massive. It measured 130 by 100 feet, much larger than many modern houses. Its walls were constructed of mud bricks and were about 10 feet thick. The size of the column bases in the center of the structure indicate that the gate probably stood between 30 and 50 feet high."

This gives us new insight to understanding the Psalm that King David wrote when he said that God was his Rock, Fortress, and High Tower. Psalm 18:2 says:

> **"The Lord is my rock, and my fortress and my deliverer; My God, my strength in whom I will trust; My buckler and the horn of my salvation, and my high tower."**

There would have been complete protection from the enemy inside the king's gate. Not only from the enemy, but also from storms that popped up that could have been life threating. And last of all from animals, thieves or assassins. God is our strong tower, from the wiles of the devil, temptation, trials and tribulations in life. His name alone is our Rock, strength, and protector.

But we see here that the king gave a command for all his servants to bow down and reverence to Haman, who was now the new prime minister of Persia. The Bible tells us here that everyone at the king's gate bowed down to him except for Mordecai. Now why is Mordecai no complying to the kings command here? Is he a troublemaker?

The answer to this is a resounding, No! He is not a troublemaker, nor is he being disobedient to King Ahasuerus either. He is directly in line with God and the law of God.

Exodus 20:4-5 "You shall not make for yourself a carved image any likeness of anything that is in heaven above or that is in the earth beneath, or that is in the water under the earth; you shall not bow down to them nor serve them. God I the Lord your God am a jealous God visiting the iniquity of the fathers upon the children to the third and fourth generation of those who hate me."

So we see that Mordecai was honoring and obeying God. His belief and conviction was obeying God's command not the command of a pagan king. He was not in violation of the king's command. Any man-made law that is made that goes against the law of God or His entire word, is a violation of His Law and Word.

The same thing happened to Daniel and his friends when they were commanded to bow down and worship the idol made by King Nebuchadnezzar. Just as Daniel was commanded not to pray to God, but too a man and another false god. But he continued to pray to God.

What about Peter, John and the other Apostles when brought before the religious leaders of their days. They were told not to teach, preach and heal in the name of Jesus. What was their reply?

Acts 5:29 "But Peter and the other apostles answered and said, "We ought to obey God rather than men."

Although we live in the year 2022, God's laws and commands are still relevant for us today; no matter what wet behind the ears, whishy washy, president, governor, Supreme Court Judge, lower court judge or lawyer says. If it goes against the law and commands of Almighty God, it is a S.I.N.! Abortion is murder. God said, "you shall not kill." Abortion is killing, it is murder, it is legalized murder. Just like marriage of homosexuals is a sin, it is not a marriage in the eyes of God. Transgender is a sin, a male changing himself into a female and a female becoming like a male.

My hat is off to Mordecai for not bowing down to this man. Way to go brother! But make no mistake about it, Mordecai as well as we will; will stick out like a sore thumb, for standing up for what we believe and for obeying God.

Notice here that all those around Mordecai at the king's gate had noticed that he was not bowing down to Haman, as commanded by the king. All those around him spoke to him every passing day about not bowing down to Haman. But when their peer pressure and coaxing him to listen and bow down did not work, they did the next best thing. They told on him to Haman, that Mordecai the Jew was not bowing to him as directed. Once they told him that he was not bowing to him they went on to say the reason for him disobeying was because he was a Jew.

Mordecai has now let the cat out of the bag. He would not allow Esther to tell everyone her true identity, but he let's them know that he was a Jew. Now I am under the impression that he did this with Esther to protect her. Because if they found out she was a Jewish young woman it could have been the death of her. So Mordecai is thinking more her safety than his own. But, later on it could still be a desperate time for them both.

Verses 5-8

"When Haman saw that Mordecai did not bow or pay him homage, Haman was filled with wrath."

"But he disdained to lay hands on Mordecai alone, for they had told him of the people of Mordecai. Instead Haman sought to destroy all the Jews who were throughout the whole kingdom of Ahasuerus-the people of Mordecai."

"In the first month, which is the month Nisan, in the twelfth year of King Ahasuerus, they cast Pur (that is, the lot), before Haman to determine the day and the month, until it fell on the twelfth month, which is the month of Adar."

Haman had not been aware of Mordecai not bowing down to him, until these people had told him. Now that he has been made aware of it, he is now going to keep a closer eye on him. Once he noticed he wasn't he just is not angry, the Bible tells us that he, "was filled with wrath." The word wrath is stronger than the word anger. It means strong vengeful anger or indignation, retributory punishment for an offense or a crime.

The Bible tells us in James 1:20 "for the wrath of man does not produce the righteousness of God." God demands of us to be righteous before Him, just as He is righteous. For example, look at Genesis chapter four. After Adam and Eve had disobeyed God and sinned by eating of the fruit He told them not to eat of, sin entered into the world. In chapter four we read about brothers Cain and Able. Once these two young men grew up, they each brought an offering to God. Cain brought an offering of the fruit of the ground and able brought of the firstborn of his flock. The Lord had accepted Abel's offering because it was the best of his flock. God rejected Cain's offering because it was not the best of his crop.

The Lord asked Cain, why he was angry at his brother. God told him in Genesis 4:7:

"If you do well, will you not be accepted? And if you do not do well, sin lies at the door. And it's desire is for you, but you should rule over it."

But God's words fell on death ears and Cain ended up killing his brother Abel.

Our anger leads us to seething, the more it seethes, it is just like a smoldering fire. At first it just smolders and puts out smoke, but the longer it smolders it turns into a flame, then it spreads into an all out, out of control blaze.

I must add here that the reason for Haman's wrath being out of control, is because his pride is hurt. This pride that he has is different that taking pride in our work and doing the best possible job. This pride is self centered pride, me, myself and I. This pride here is the type of pride that got the devil kicked out of heaven, read Isaiah 14:12-15. In Proverbs 16:18 the Bible says, **"Pride goes before destruction, and haughtiness before a fall."** That's what happened to Cain, that is what happened to Satan, that is what happened to Nabal. Eventually Satan's pride will one day come to a full end, when Jesus Christ our Lord and Savior cast him into Lake of Fire. He will be tormented day and night forever and ever.

3: Promotion of a Wicked Man

You know people like this are to be pitied, because they are not as happy as they put on. I mean, I really feel sad for people like Haman. The reason I do is because they choose to live a life without God. Don't get me wrong, we may be saved but we still get mad and angry. The one difference is, the Holy Spirit will convict us about being angry towards others until we repent of being angry. However, people like Haman never get over it.

Let's look at Galatians 5:22-23 at fruit of people like Haman. But, let's not forget that before we came to know Christ, we too acted just like them. Probably still do because we are in construction not a completed project yet until we arrive home with the Lord. But here is the fruit of evil doers:

"Now the works of the flesh are evident, which are:
1. Adultrey
2. Fornifcation
3. Uncleaness
4. Lewdness
5. Idolatry
6. Sorcery
7. Hatred*
8. Contentious*
9. Jealousies*
10. Outburst of wrath*
11. Self Ambitions*
12. Dissensions*
13. Heresies
14. Envy*
15. Murders*
16. Drunkness
17. Revelries*
"and the like; of which I tell you beforehand, just as I also told you in time past, that those who practice such things will not inherit the kingdom of God."

If you noticed I placed asterisks besides the ones that fit to Haman. He wasn't a man of God, he practiced evil everyday of his life. He should have been a bigger man than this, allowing one man to up end his life because he didn't bow to him. He's the Prime Minister of the land, and he is getting all mad and bent out of shape because Mordecai isn't bowing to him. Well right now he's filled with wrath but let's take a look at what else is taking place within him.

In the King James Version of verse six, it says, **"And he thought scorn to lay hands on Mordecai alone."** The New King James Version says, **"But he disdained to lay hands on Mordecai alone,"** I like how the Living Bible writes this verse, **"Haman was furious but decided not to lay hands on Mordecai alone, but to move against all of Mordecai's people, the Jews."**

The words scorn and disdain mean the same- open dislike and disrespect or mockery often mixed with indignation. Haman just didn't hate and have contempt towards Mordecai only, but this wrathful indignation of his was towards all the Jews. He wanted to kill all of the Jews including Mordecai along with them. His idea was to rid the entire kingdom of them. This was nothing more than genocide, of the entire nation of Israel.

There is only one problem with Haman's plan, and it is this! God will not allow it to happen! Haman is not fighting against the Jews here, he has now positioned himself on God's battle field. We know that God will not allow this because of God's promise to Abraham in Genesis 12.

> *Genesis 12:1-3 NKJV "Now the had said to Abram, "Get out of your country from your family and from your fathers house, to a land that I will show you. I will make you a great nation; I will bless you and make your name great; and you shall be a blessing. I will bless those who bless you, and I will curse him who curses you; and all the families of the earth shall be blessed."*

> *Zechariah 2:8 "For thus saith the Lord of Hosts; After the glory hath he sent me unto the nations which spoiled you: for he that toucheth you toucheth apple of his eye."*

God's promise to Abraham was to make him into a great nation and He has done that. The Greatest Blessing to come from the nation of Israel is the Messiah Jesus Christ, the Son of the Living God. God made it clear that whoever cursed Abraham and his seed they would be cursed. But whoever blessed them would be blessed.

3: Promotion of a Wicked Man

America has benefited and prospered throughout the years because she has been good to Israel. In fact, America is the only country that has been good to the nation of Israel and the Jews.

We know of a little two by squirt, that wore a little mustache the same size of his brain; that tried to annihilate the Jews but his plans failed. He and his Nazi Army killed around six million Jews, but yet the Jews are still with us. Why? Because of God's promise to Abraham, and because Israel is the apple of God's eye. A

As for Hitler and his bunch, they're no longer with us today, but the Jews are and so is the nation of Israel. Many have tired in the past to exterminate the people of Israel but has failed. Call me what you will but I truly do love the Jewish people and pray for them everyday. Yes I am proud to be a Christian a follower of Jesus Christ and I am proud to be a supporter of Israel.

Last of all I see this as end time prophecy against the nation of Israel, as well as end time prophecy against the Church. Both of them together are under the protection of God Almighty and will be until the end. Our enemy is the devil, he has the same contempt against the church as Haman does against the Jews. The devil would love nothing more than to destroy the Church, but he can't, because Christ will not allow it.

The write of Esther is very detailed in his writing of the book. I like it because he gives us the month when Haman was plotting his genocide as well as the number of years of King Ahasuerus' reign. It took place during the twelfth year of King Ahasuerus' reign, Haman begins to plot his plan by wicked devices. Remember Galatians 5:22-23, one of the fruits of the flesh is sorcery.

The month was Nisan, which is the first month of the Jewish Calendar. The pulpit commentary says this; *"This name was first given to the month by the Jews after the return from the captivity. It was the Babylonian name of the first maonth of the years and supersede the old Jewish name, Abib."*

The first time we read about this month "Abib" is in Exodus 12, the Bible says this:

Exodus 12:2 *"This month shall be unto you the beginning of months: it shall be the first month of the year to you."*

God had told Moses and Aaron that He was doing something new for them and with them. Their days of slavery has been brought to and end, they have been liberated By God, for God. This month was the first month, the month of Abib.

So, what happened on this night? This was the night that all the Jews celebrated the very first Passover. They were to prepare bread without yeast, and a lamb. They placed the blood of the lamb on the doorpost, that night for when the Lord passed over and seen the blood on the doorpost everyone inside was safe. If there was no blood on the doorpost or outside the house then they would be killed if they were the first born. But as for the Egyptians there was no blood and death came to all the first born of both man and beast.

Then we move ahead almost fifteen hundred years later, we have another new beginning in the month Abib. That's right, we see Jesus in the upper room with His disciples having the Last Supper, which is the Passover. Jesus Christ was that Passover Lamb, who would be crucified the next morning on the cross. This would be the night of His illegal arrest, desertion of His disciples, false accusations, unjust trials, slapped, hit in the face with fist, hit in the head with a club, beat with a whip, sentenced to die on the old rugged cross, between two criminals. So the month of Abib corresponds to March and April here in America. It is when we celebrate the death, burial and resurrection of Jesus Christ.

This took place in Ahasuerus' twelfth year of reign, so nearly five years has passed since he took Esther to be his wife and new Queen. So all of this has been building for some time now and has now reached a climax.

The next thing we see mentioned here is the word PUR is used here. It means to cast lots. So they cast lots which was like rolling the dice to determine the month and the day when the massacre of the Jews would take place. The Jews now celebrate this day every year, but it is called Purim. It is celebrated in the month Adar on the fourteenth and fifteenth of the month.

Haman and his magician friends cast these lots for every month beginning with the month Nisan or (Abib). They went through each month of the year to determine which month was the lucky month to carry out his plan of killing all the Jews. So after going through each month of casting lots it fell on the month of Adar. I believe that God was at work in this sinister scheme of this wicked man Haman. I believe that it was God, that caused the lots to fall upon

3: Promotion of a Wicked Man

this date and month. Because He was giving it plenty of time for everything to unfold, to be found out in His timing.

The casting of lots was a very common practice in the east. It is mentioned forty seven time in the Bible. The casting of lots was a means of determining the will of God. This can be found in Leviticus 16:8 (from Wikipedia)

"Then Aaron shall cast lots for the two goats: on lot for the Lord and the other lot for the scapegoat."

In Joshua 18:10, Joshua cast sacred lots to determine which tribe should have each section of land in the Promise Land.

Then in Jonah 1:7, the sailors cast lots to see whose (gods) was responsible for the storm they were in. This lot fell on Jonah, because the God he served and worshiped was the one who brought it. The (gods) they served were idols, there was no way their (gods) could bring about anything at all.

Last of all, the Roman soldiers cast lots for Jesus garments, in Matthew 27:35. This was done by rolling something like dice or drawing straws. Many of us know about drawing straws because we did it sometimes while growing up. There was five of us, there would be five pieces of small sticks, but one would be shorter than the other. One person would mix them up, hold them in their hands as if by equal size. Whoever chose the short stick, then the lot fell on them, to do something.

But like I said before, God is in control of these lots. Many times, we may be so arrogant to believe we are the ones in control, but we are not, God is. God and God alone made the lots to fall on the month Adar. He did this to give this evil plan, time to be found out.

The month these lots fell on was the month Adar. This is the last month of the year counting from Nisan. This month has twenty-nine days in it. On our calendar it would be February and March. Adar is the happiest, most joyous month of the Hebrew Calendar. In fact, it's motto is "When Adar comes, joy is increased. (from Rediscover the Classic NCSY Works by, Rabbi Aryeh Kaplan)

Verses 8-11

"Then Haman said to King Ahasuerus, "There is a certain people scattered and dispersed among the people in all the provinces of

your kingdom; their laws are different from all other people's, and they do not keep the king's laws. Therefore it is not fitting for the king to let them remain."

If it pleases the king, let a decree be written that they be destroyed, and I will pay ten thousand talents of silver into the hands of those who do the work, to bring it into the king's treasuries."

"So the king took his signet ring from his hand and gave it to Haman, the son of Hammedatha the Agagite, the enemy of the Jews."

And the king said to Haman, "The money and the people are given to you, to do with them as seems good to you."

Now that the date and month have been determined, Haman took it a step further in his plan. That next step was proposing it to the king for his authorization and approval. If you notice he tells the king that there is a certain people, he did not tell the king that they were the Jews living throughout his kingdom. So apparently, the Jews were scattered through out the one hundred and twenty-seven provinces. There were at least forty thousand Jews who had returned to their native land of Israel. Upon their arrival in their homeland, the walls were rebuilt and so was the temple.

The next thing we see him telling the king, is that their laws and their religion was different from all the other peoples and nations in his kingdom. He took it further by telling a lie that they do not obey his laws and commands. No, it was only Mordecai who the Bible points out that was not bowing to Haman. The other thing was this; the Persian kings allowed the nation they defeated to practice their religion. They often took and learned of their religions and sometimes worshiped their god's.

This isn't the first time nor the last time that someone had come against the Jews with similar accusations. We find it in the Books of Nehemiah, Ezra, Daniel almost word for word. My question is this, "Does any of this sound familiar for us today?" Has there not been laws made that we cannot express our beliefs on certain laws that have been made?

But King Ahasuerus does something here that takes me by surprise. He does ask any questions about this at all. To me he does things without thinking,

3: Promotion of a Wicked Man

and nonchalantly gives things his permission to accomplish things. That's one reason I believe he lost to the Greeks, as well as banishing Vashti as queen. He is giving this ego maniac more power to accomplish his motives.

Before I go on further, let me explain to you what a signet ring was. A signet ring according to Webster Dictionary was a finger ring engraved with a signet, seal, or a monogram. This ring he gave to Haman had either King Ahasuerus' initials on it, or some sort of sign or symbol that was recognized by everyone that, it was his signature. They were pressed into warm soft wax that left the impression on the ring in the wax.

With Ahasuerus giving Haman this ring is like giving a thief the keys to every store in your town. Or it would be like giving the most hardened murder the key to a gun store. In this case the king was giving the Jews enemy the go ahead to destroy everyone of them. This kind of power in the hands of Haman is not a good thing for the Jews, in the kingdom of Ahasuerus.

If you notice here as well that the king has no, and I mean no respect for human life at all here. Throughout the times of the Old Testament days until now; there is still no respect for human life in the Middle East. Take a look at Iran who is always speaking out about exterminating the Nation of Israel. This is not only sad, but it is very dangerous not just for Israel, but the world as a whole.

Notice here to that Haman is willing to use his own money to carry out the plan to destroy them. In the Living Bible, it says, **"I will pay $20,000,000 into the royal treasury for the expenses involved in this purge."** He must have been a very rich man in order to offer this much money to have them destroyed. But here in verse nine he only mentions this amount of money, he never gave it to be done. The reason why; is because in verse eleven the king tells him to put away his money but to take it from his royal bank account. Not only is the money given to him, but the people meaning his army would work with him in the destruction of these people.

Man has not changed at all when it comes to having great wealth. The more we make the more we spend. Some people not all who are rich are scallywag's, who think they can get away with anything, just because they are rich. However, there are people making money hand over fist, through porn, drug trafficking, human trafficking and so on. Like I said, they have no respect for human life at all, only money matters to them.

The Bible tells us in 1 Timothy 6:

1 Timothy 6:10 "For the love of money is the root of all evil. And some people craving money have wandered from the true faith and pierced themselves with many sorrows."

Money isn't evil, it's the love of money that makes it evil. Therefore, the money here is being used for evil, it is being used to murder an entire nation of people. There is blood money in America! That blood money is the money allotted to or donated to abortions to be performed on innocent defenseless unborn babies.

One thing that I noticed here about the kings of Persia is how gullible they were. The reason I say that is because in the Book of Daniel, King Darius had Daniel thrown into the lion's den because his servants lied to him about Daniel. Think about it! He is just taking Haman at his word and has not investigated this as he did against his two bodyguards who planned to kill him. Just like Darius took his servants words that Daniel was breaking the law. So now he has the licenses to kill all the Jews throughout the land.

Verses 12-15

"Then the king's scribes were called on the thirteenth day of the first month, and a decree was written according to all that Haman commanded-to the king's satraps, to the governors who were over each province, to the officials of all people, to every province according to its script, and to every people in their language. In the name of King Ahasuerus it was written, and sealed with the king's signet ring."

"And the letters were sent by couriers into all the king's provinces, to destroy, to kill, and to annihilate all the Jews, both young and old, little children and women, in one day, on the thirteenth day of the twelfth month, which is the month of Adar, and to plunder their possessions."

"A copy of the document was to be issued as law in every province, being published for all people, that they should be ready for that day."

3: Promotion of a Wicked Man

"The couriers went out, hastened by the king's command; and the decree was proclaimed in Shushan the citadel. So the king and Haman sat down to drink, but the city of Shushan was perplexed."

The king's scribes were called in on this day to write this decree. A scribe is a person who copies out documents, especially one employed to do this before printing was invented. (From Oxford Dictionary.) In ancient Israel, Scribes where learned men whose business was to study the Law, transcribe it, and write commentaries on it. They were also hired on occasions when the need for a written document arose or when an interpretation of a legal point was needed. Ezra, "a teacher well versed in the Law of Moses," was a scribe Ezra 7:6. (from Got Questions.Com) In Jesus day the Scribes, Pharisees and Sadducees were always contradicting what Jesus said, preached on, or healing someone or doing something on the Sabbath.

Haman was not allowing any grass to grow under his feet. Let's get this done and lets get it done today. Which was the thirteenth day of Adar, when the scribes came in to him and took down everything he said that needed to be done; and the month, day, and time it was to be done. After this was completed in writing and made into law, it was to be sent to all the officials who ruled under the king. Notice here that it uses the name Satraps. These people were a provincial governor in ancient Persian empire.

Try to think of it like this, in our day and time. King Ahasuerus would be President, Haman Vice President, then all the 127 Satraps would be like the governors of each state in the United States. So each letter that was copied down had to be written in the language of each nation, tribe in his entire province. That is a whole lot of hand writing that needed to be done. Once that was done then it had the blessing of the king, from Haman using his signet ring making it chiseled in stone, it was now a law.

Here in verse thirteen, I learned something new and very interesting. It is the very first part of verse thirteen. **"And the letters were sent by posts into all the kings provinces."** Thanks to King Darius, he had good roads made and had created these posts throughout the land, which is just like the Pony Express that was used in America; from 1860-1861. Only expert riders rode these horses to another post, exchanged the mail into the hands of a fresh rider on a fresh horse. This was the way the mail was delivered to the 127 provinces.

This mail was different because in this letter it was the death sentence of the Jews. This reminds me of another time when a letter of death was delivered to kill someone. That was when King David had Uriah, the Hittite killed. He had written it to his commanding office Joab, to place Uriah in the hottest part of the war. Uriah the Hittite carried his own death sentence to Joab that day. And that is exactly what Joab did, and Uriah the Hittite died.

At this point the Jews are unaware of the law and the letters going out to kill them all. Notice that the Bible tells us, *"to destroy, to kill, and to annihilate all the Jews, both young and old, little children and women, in one day, on the thirteenth day of the twelfth month, which is the month Adar, and to plunder their possessions."* Although some of them are unaware of the law to destroy all of them, God is aware of it. He sees all and He knows all! He knew this day was coming even before He created the world and put everything in motion. We can never ever hide from God nor can we hide anything from Him. We know this because, Adam and Eve tried hiding but God knew exactly where to find them.

It did not matter how old they were, it didn't matter if they were man or woman or child. If they were a known to be a Jew, it was going to be lights out for all of them. Not only was this bringing an end to the nation of Israel as a whole, but everything they owned would be taken as plunder.

This is the very reason I titled this, "God Watches From the Shadows." Because as stated before, God's name is not mentioned, and just because His name doesn't appear; doesn't mean He is silent or uncaring. No it is just the opposite, He is always there. Before the storm comes, when it comes, during the storm. That's when I compared this Book to what took place in Mark 6:45-50.

Jesus had just feed the 5,000 men, besides the number of women and children. After performing this miracle, they took up twelve baskets of what was left over. Jesus made his disciples leave at once by boat to go over to Bethsaida, while He was sending the people back home. But then He went on top of a mountain to pray to His Father.

Evening time came upon them, while they were in the middle of the sea, and Jesus was alone on the land. That's when He looked out and seen them struggling against the wind to row the boat. I love that part of the story. He often stands of in the distance, not to far away from us, watching over us. Just like the times I have kept my eyes on my children, watching them, to see what they will do when I am not in sight of them. Like the time I took our son deer hunting, I wasn't very far from him, but he thought I wasn't around at all. I watched how he handled the rifle, and how he did not touch it until he seen a deer.

But notice that Jesus came to them out on the water, around about three o'clock in the morning. He would have passed them up until they seen Him walking on the water, thinking He was a ghost. But then he spoke to them, **"Be of good cheer! It is I ;do not be afraid."** Man, I love this! This is good stuff here folks! God is always, always watching over us, and all the events taking place in the world. Today, it looks like that nuclear war could break out in milliseconds. But it will not happen until God says that it can happen.

The closing verses we see that all of these copies had been made for all the provinces. Now that they have that work done it is now time to deliver all the copies to each province. This way it could be read, given to the people everywhere in his kingdom, to be ready for this day of destroying the Jews.

This would be equal to what took place during the American Revolution. They had what was called Minute Men. These men were volunteers to be ready in a minute's notice. The king and Haman wanted this date to be etched into their minds, and to start their killing of the Jews on this day. So these post were sent out, but they were hastened by the king to hurry it up and get it done.

Then once again we see the king and Haman drinking together. Both of them had hard hearts, because while they are drinking and living it up; news is being carried to kill people in cold blood. This is no different from the things that take place in our nation or other nations. We have leaders all over the world who are living in the lap of luxury while they starve their own people or kill them for some trumped up charge.

All of this goes back to having a personal relationship with Jesus Christ. This is the most important thing in the life of people today, but so many chose to reject Him and push Him away.

Haman has created chaos in the citadel of Shushan. Everything was peaceful and good, but now just like the devil, he has brought about fear, hate, evil and death. Whose side are you on today? Are you on the devil's side? Or are you on the Lord's side.

J. Thomas Ruble II

4

Evil Plans of a Wicked Man Revealed

Verses 1-3

"When Mordecai learned all that had happened, he tore his clothes and put on sackcloth and ashes, and went out into the midst of the city. He cried out with a loud and bitter cry."

"He went as far as the front of the king's gate, for no one might enter the king's gate clothed with sackcloth."

"And in every province where the king's command and decree arrived there was great mourning among the Jews, with fasting, weeping, and wailing; and many lay in sackcloth and ashes."

Mordecai had become aware of the edict, that had come from the king to destroy all the Jews. Once he realized the extreme danger of all the Jews, throughout the entire province of the king. He tore his clothes, put on sackcloth and put ashes on himself from head to foot. This act of tearing ones clothes and putting on sackcloth and ashes was a very common act for those who lived in the Middle East. It also was a very common act performed by the Jews. The tearing or ripping of ones clothing was a sign of mourning, grief and loss. (from Got Questions.Com)

There were many men from the Bible who tore their clothes and wore sackcloth and ashes. The one that is very familiar to all of us is the man Job, in chapter one of the book that is given his name. Job was a man who had lost everything, from his children, servants, livestock as well ash boils on his body.

When all of these troubles came upon him, he tore his clothes, put on sackcloth and ashes.

Sackcloth and ashes were used in the Old Testament times as a symbol of debasement, mourning and or repentance. (Got Questions.com) So we see here that Mordecai is showing mourning, grief, and suffering deep within his soul.

Another time is when the people of Nineveh, had heard the message of the reluctant Prophet Jonah. When they heard of the impending doom that God was bringing unless they repented. They all put sackcloth upon themselves as well as their animals and fasted. Upon doing this He showed mercy and grace and spared the entire city from being destroyed.

So just what is sackcloth? What is it made of? Sackcloth was a coarse material usually made of black goat's hair, making it quite uncomfortable to wear. The ashes signified desolation and ruin. (Got Questions.com)

After putting on sackcloth and ashes, he went to the middle of the city of Shushan. So now everyone can see Mordecai and the shape that he is in, that he is in distress and mourning. As he went along, he was crying out with bitter and mournful cries. These mournful cries were loud, and death-defying cries that could be heard a long way off.

From this verse it is almost as if, the writer is painting us a picture of this taking place from the pages. It's as if we ourselves can see him and hear him in his distress of pain and grief. I believe that the entire citadel, as well as the entire palace could hear him wailing as he walked through. I believe these cries of his was very shrill.

He walked through the citadel, all the way to the front of the king's gate and stopped. The reason for this is because no one was allowed to enter the king's gate dressed in sackcloth, because it was despised. Once he arrived there he sat down and kept grieving for the action taken against his people.

But in verse three we see that Mordecai is not alone in his mourning process. Because all the Jews throughout the entire provinces had also dressed themselves in sackcloth and ashes, mourned with fasting, weeping and wailing. This must have been a very sad sight to behold and hear, with Jews everywhere doing this. There had to be at least a hundred and fifty thousand people, maybe more sitting down and crying out.

4: Evil Plans of a Wicked Man Revealed

It makes me think of all the Christians around the world today, who mourn and grieve over the things that takes place. How many of us mourn over lost souls, famines, devastation from war, earthquakes, innocent people murdered, abortion, homosexual marriage and so on? How about how our country is torn asunder because of politics, news media pitting people against each other? Our country just is not divided, our country is shattered! The Bible tells us:

"And if one member suffers, all the members suffer with it; or if one member is honored all the members rejoice with it."

All the Jews throughout the provinces were suffering together, as well as all Christians suffer together. When a member of the Church as a whole suffers, we all suffer with that member as they are suffering. This holds true for those whose family member has died, bad news of cancer or some fatal disease, persecution, or addictions. These things grieve us because we live in a fallen world, we're fallen people and we see the results of sin in the world as well as our own sins.

Take for example of what is taking place in Ukraine for the past six months of war with Russia. It grieves us to see the evil and cruelty of a man who does not regard life. President Putin's Army has massacred innocent lives because of his greed and hate. Some news footage showed one of his Army tanks deliberately running over a car with a person inside, leaving dead bodies strewn over the streets of Mariupol.

Notice here to that this verse here mentions the word fasting. As I stated before, fasting is a way of humbling ourselves before God. Throughout the Bible fasting and prayer are linked together like links in a chain. Although prayer is not mentioned here, I believe they were praying to God. Notice also here in the Book of Esther the is no prophet of God telling them to fast and pray. They did not go to a prophet to ask what they should do next. They took it upon themselves to fast before Almighty God.

If you go back to the book of Judges up to this point in Esther, the Children of Israel had been disobedient to God. They had spent several hundreds of years worshipping idols and killing their children in sacrifices to idols. God had sent His prophets to warn them and to steer them back onto the right path. But they would not humble themselves before Almighty God, until the day the Northern Kingdom Israel was taken over by the Assyrians. Then the

Southern Kingdom of Judah was taken over by Babylon for seventy years of captivity. Now we see them fasting.

Fasting is going without anything to eat for a period of time. Sometimes they went without food for a few days, a week or weeks, or at times as many as forty days. In Exodus 34 we see that Moses went without food for forty days and forty nights.

> ***Exodus 34:28 "She was there with the LORD forty days and forty nights; he neither ate bread nor drank water. And He wrote on the tablets the words of the covenant, the Ten Commandments."***

Jesus also went without food for forty days and forty nights, during His time in the wilderness being tempted of the devil; Matthew 4:2:

> ***"And when He had fasted forty days and forty nights, afterward He was hungry."***

It has been discovered that fasting for short periods of times has been associated with a wide array of potential health benefits, including weight loss, as well as improved blood sugar control, heart health, brain function and cancer preventions. (www.healthline.com)

The next thing we see them doing is they are weeping. They were crying their eyes out as we would say today. Maybe they were reminded of the weeping Prophet Jeremiah who wept over his people because of his love for them. He wept over them because of their sins, and the foreboding doom that awaited them. Jesus, our Lord and Savior wept over Jerusalem, because of their disbelief in Himself before raising Lazarus from the dead. He even wanted to gather them together as a hen does her chicks, to hold them in loving protection.

Today there is no weeping, when there should be weeping because of the sins of the world and our nation. We should be weeping over our sins as well as the sin taking place in the world and the church. We should be weeping over lost sinners and those who have perished. Many times, I have sat in our living room during Bible Study and just wept over the things taking place in the world. Many is the time I have cried just sitting on our porch and seeing people walk by drunk or high. Many times, I have wept because I have reached out to them to accept Christ as Lord and Savior of their lives, but they do not want to change. Many times, as a child until now I cried, because of how our family treated each other, and has disowned each other because of pity differences.

Last of all we can see how deeply moved they are from the depths of their souls, because of the wailing they were doing. To wail or wailing means to express sorrow audibly. This comes with great pain deep within us. I can remember the day our grandfather died. At first I had tears, then all at once a deep groaning within myself that came with a very great shout of pain. I screamed, yelled, hit the wall with my fist. It was a very painful ordeal to take that death had come to him.

To be honest with you, the day of 911 was an experience like this. It was very painful for me to take in, knowing our nation had been attacked. There were days it was so painful that I drove to the farm were we grew up, walked in the woods and just screamed. Then just cry and pray to God to help me with the pain and to heal our nation. Then this Bible verse came to me, from Psalms 34:18:

> ***"The Lord is near to those who have a broken heart, and saves such as have a contrite spirit."***

I didn't see a vision of angels, nor did I see the Lord, but His presence was there. It was as if He took me into His arms and held me as I just cried. Sometimes crying and wailing is good for cleansing the soul.

Closing thought on this. I began to think about how that when Jesus began His message on the Sermon on the Mount. If maybe, He was thinking about this taking place here in these first three verses of Esther. Blessed are they that mourn for they shall be comforted. Blessed are the meek, for they shall inherit the earth. They were being all of these things here. He may have or may not have been thinking about this time period in the life of Mordecai and Esther. But we see that the Jews throughout the entire provinces are suffering together. I believe that it is time for Christians all over the world to come together; in sackcloth and ashes within our souls and to mourn over our sins, to repent and start being doers of His Word as well as we hear it.

Verses 4-5

So Esther's maids and eunuchs came and told her, and the queen was deeply distressed. Then she sent garments to clothe Mordecai and take his sackcloth away from him, but he would not accept them.

Then Esther called Hathach, one of the king's eunuchs whom he had appointed to attend her, and she gave him a command concerning Mordecai, to learn what and why this was.

Although Esther lived in the palace, she probably did not know of the edict, that was made by Haman and the king. Remember she is living in a different room in the palace from the king, and she can only be near him when he calls for her. But now she is about to become aware of the law that was made to eliminate her people and herself. Also keep in mind that she still has not made it known that she is a Jewish woman. The only thing that her maidens and eunuchs know is that she and Mordecai are related. Don't forget that while Esther was in the beauty contest, Mordecai visited her everyday to see how she was doing. Also, they knew that he sat at the king's gate as well, being a servant of the king. So, they tell her that Mordecai was in distress and was wearing sackcloth and ashes.

When She heard this news about Mordecai, the Bible tells us that she was exceedingly grieved, in the King James Version, the New King James Version says she was deeply distressed. This tells us that she was extremely painful for what she had heard about Mordecai. I believe there is two ways of looking at this for what she was going through. Frist, she knew that he was suffering over something, and she was hurting because he was hurting. Second, it could be that it was somewhat of and embarrassment to her for how he was acting. To be truthful about the matter, she really doesn't know why he is acting like this. Things can't be that bad, after all she was the Queen and had been now for five years.

Then notice that she has sent him some new clean clothes to put on and for him to remove the sackcloth and ashes. More than likely these clothes were very bright and colorful, as well as expensive coming from the palace. He was to take off the sackcloth and to put on the clean clothes she sent. Then take the sackcloth and discard it somewhere.

Often times our way of thinking gets us into trouble. Sometimes we put our best foot forward to help someone, but they don't need our help. We get in the way, when sometimes it's better to leave them alone. I believe the same way the Pulpit Commentary and J. Vernon McGee writes, that she sort of took this matter lighthearted. Mordecai figuratively speaking has a gaping stomach wound and needs a doctor. But Esther did not know the size of the wound and sent him a Band-Aid.

A good example of this is when someone's family member or friend has died. We don't know exactly how they are feeling or grieving, because everyone grieves differently. They may be silent, be a recluse, cry a lot, they'll lash out at us, become angry or even violent. But who are we to say to them they shouldn't do these things. They're in need of a doctor for the gushing wound they have deep within their souls. The only doctor who can cure this pain is the Lord Himself.

But the thing about it is often times they don't want to hear this. I remember B.R. Lakin saying, "The only thing a rabid dog needs is water, but it don't want water! The Word of God is the water, but people don't want it." We have to be careful and gather all the facts before we rush in to help them, and most of all pray about it first. Let's not forget about the three friends of Job and how they rushed in and told him that he had sinned against God because of the troubles he was going through. Job told them in Job 16:2, **"I have heard many such things: miserable comforters are you all!"** My wife and I attended a church where a woman ended up getting cancer, and another woman in the church told her, that she brought this upon herself because of her past sins. Really!

To this day I am very careful and still don't know what to say to someone, when a love one dies, finds out about cancer or some other form of deadly disease. All I can think of saying is "I'm so sorry. I love you." Then embrace them with a hug.

There was a time when I worked at a factory making trailer axel's for semi-trucks. We had a young lady who was nineteen years old who worked with us. Everyday she came to work, she was yelling and screaming out profanity. She used enough profanity in one hour, for everyone and the factory next door.

Even those who used profanity was wore down listening to her day in and day out.

After several weeks of this it was draining people's morale. They came to me one day and said, "Preacher," do you hear what she is saying. I acknowledged them that I had and how could I not. Then that is when they requested that I talk to her about her profanity. I told them to go talk to her, but they scattered like roaches with a light coming on.

So, I had had enough of hearing her everyday as well as them complaining about it everyday. So, I walked down to the line she was on, while both lines were on break. She was setting there all by herself because no one wanted to be around her. I said hello to her and began talking small talk with her, then I got right to the root of the problem. I asked her about her family life and married life. Just then she opened up to me. Telling me about her mom being from a charismatic denomination, always cramming religion down her throat, telling her she was going to hell. Then her dad was an alcoholic, drank all the time, and neither one ever told her that they loved her. And they had divorced and remarried each other at least four times.

At the age of fourteen she had sex, was pregnant at sixteen, married and divorced two times and was only nineteen years old. She proceeds telling me more things about her life and as she did, I noticed that her facial expression changed as well as tears welling up in her eyes. The next thing I know she was crying hard, and said, "I just want to be loved!" Now I had tears in my eyes. She came up to me and just put her arms around me and I put mine around her. She kept crying and I told her, "Jesus loves you, I love you. Stop living life for the wrong reasons and accept Jesus as your Savior." We talked a little longer and she received Jesus as her savior that day. From then on she was quite as a church mouse, and had a joyful expression on her face everyday.

At the end of verse four here we read that Mordecai did not accept the clothes that Esther had sent him. There was a very good reason for doing this is because there is danger ahead for the Jews everywhere through out the entire kingdom. This would be sending a signal to Esther that there was something definitely very wrong.

When Esther received word that Mordecai would not accept the clothes she sent him. She then sent Hathach not to ask Mordecai what was wrong but commanded him to tell him what was wrong. Queen Esther was wanting answers and wanting them now.

Verses 6- 9

So Hathach went out to Mordecai in the city square that was in front of the king's gate.

And Mordecai told him all that had happened to him, and the sum of money that Haman had promised to pay into the king's treasuries to destroy the Jews.

He also gave hi a copy of the written decree for their destruction, which was given at Shushan, that he might show it to Esther and explain it to her, and that he might command her to go in to the king to make supplication to him and plead before him for her people.

So Hathach returned and told Esther the words of Mordecai.

Before going on further, I want to give you the pronuncion of this eunuch's name. It is pronounced Hay Tack. He was an official who had been appointed by the king to manage over Queen Esther.

I would say the reason she sent Hathach to Mordecai instead of going herself, was because she was the queen. So she is sending him in her place as her messenger. She is wanting him to find out why Mordecai is acting like this and what is wrong?

Today in America we have delegates who serve us on the national level all the way down to the state level. They are there to listen to the people and to carry out the demands of the people, providing it is lawful. But today, some, not all do not listen to the pepole, because they want to be self serving.

Instead of using wisdom and righteous judgment, they say and do things to please others so they can get elected again. It seems the more sinful things we demand are right in their eyes; but when it comes to demanding Godly things, well, that outdated and senseless.

Once he arrives at the king's gate where Mordecai is sitting, he ask him what Queen Esther wanted to know. So, in layman terms, Mordecai "Lets it rip!" So, he begins telling him everything and the reason he was grieving in sackcloth. It was because he had not bowed down to Haman when he passed by as the king had commanded. And how Haman had used his money to bribe the king in order to bring about this demise to the Jews. To put the icing on the cake He hands Hathach the copy of the decree that had given the order to kill all the Jews in the entire province. He gave it to Hathach so that he could give it to Esther so that she could she it for herself. Here's the evidence Esther, I present you with exhibit A. As we would say in the country, "This is the proof in the pudding!"

Remember during the beauty contest, she was to keep quite about her identity and her people. But now he is telling her to let the cat out of the bag, because this just doesn't concern him, it's in her best interest to let the king know that his queen is a Jewish woman.

These verses remind me of our Lord Jesus. How? Well Haman had offered a bribe to the king to kill all the Jews. The religious leaders of Jesus' day offered a bribe to anyone who would betray Jesus. We all know that Judas ended up betraying Him for thirty pieces of silver.

They made a decree upon His life, to snub Him out, kill Him, get rid of Him once and for all. They were jealous of Him and His ministry, because pepole were following Him and not them. But how can you get rid of the Son of God, who is, and was God. You can't! He was fully God and fully human. He can die a death like us, but no grave can hold him down. Why? Because He was fully God and He and only He has power over everything including death and the grave.

So notice that Queen Esther is an advocate for her people. This is the reason God has place her in this position at this very moment. Jesus Christ is our Advocate before the Father.

So now Esther now knows the reason for Mordecai's actions. Now she can react to this and plan accordingly, through wisdom and virtue.

Verses 10-12

Then Esther spoke to Hathach, and gave him a command for Mordecai:

"All the king's servants and the people of the kings provinces know that any man or woman who goes into the inner court to the king,

4: Evil Plans of a Wicked Man Revealed

who has not been called, he has but one law: put all to death, except the one to whom the king holds out the golden scepter, that he may live. Yet I myself have not been called to go in to the king these thirty days."

So they told Mordecai Esther's words.

Now that Esther knows what is taking place, she gives Mordecai this command that she has given to Hathach. She is answering Mordecai's response that she should go in before the king to make a plea for her people. She is reminding Mordecai that everyone in the king's province know that there is a law that no one; man or woman cannot just walk into the inner court where the king is unless the king calls that individual. In other words, King Ahasuerus does not have an open-door policy. This is pretty bad when your wife the queen has to have the king make an appointment for her to visit him.

However, this reminds me of Exodus twenty-four. What took place in this chapter happened before the tabernacle was built. God told Moses to bring his brother Aaron, his sons Nadab and Abihu and the seventy elders of Israel to worship the Lord from afar. Moses alone was the only one to come near to the Lord, and no one else was to come with him.

In Leviticus the Bible tells us:

***Leviticus 16:2** "And the Lord said to Moses, "Tell your brother Aaron not to enter freely into the Most Holy place behind the veil in front of the Mercy Seat on the Ark or else he will die, because I appear in the cloud above the mercy seat."*

Aaron was the high priest of Israel, but he just couldn't walk into the Holy of Holies whenever he wanted to. This was a special time God had set apart for him. If he just walked into where the Ark was before the time God appointed, he would have died. But before he could even enter, he had to cleanse himself through sacrifice of sins before entering.

So since Aaron was the only one to enter once a year when appointed, meant that NO ONE, but him was allowed in this inner room. I must tell you this also, that there was a very thick veil that covered the entrance to this room. That means that there was a barrier between God and the people.

If anyone broke God's laws or commandments, the result was death. Look what happened to Nadab and Abihu, Aaron's two sons who disobeyed God in Leviticus 10:1-2. The same was true for everyone in the province of Ahasuerus. If they just walked into him without him asking for them was to be or could have been instant death to them. There was only one way to escape from being killed and that is if and when he called or if and when he held out the golden scepter.

This scepter is probably a staff or a short rod. As a symbol of authority, the use of the scepter originated in the idea that the ruler was a shepherd of his people. Genesis 49:10; Numbers 24:17; Psalm 45:6; Isaiah 14:5. (from Easton's Bible Dictionary)

When the king held out this golden scepter to the person(s) who entered his inner room; this was his way of showing mercy and his acceptance of that person(s). If and this is a pretty big if. If he holds it out this golden scepter to Queen Esther, then her life will be spared. If he does not hold it out to her then she could very well be killed by the king. This is the big question standing out in Esther's mind, "Would he hold it out to her? Or would he not hold it out to her?" Let's not forget that we have a king here that is drinking most of the time, he's got a short temper, and he has banished his former Queen Vashti.

Let's not ignore this or pass over this to quickly over the golden scepter. Let's look at Numbers 24:17:

> ***"I see Him, but not here now. I perceive Him but far in the distant future. A Star will rise from Jacob; a Scepter will emerge from Israel. It will crush the head's of Moab's people, cracking the skulls of the people of Sheth."***

Who is this verse speaking about here? This verse is speaking about Christ! He was God's Son, the Star that came from Jacob. He was God's Scepter, the mercy and grace, of Almighty God. God held out His Son on the cross sacrificing His Son in our place for our sins. Through His death we are offered pardon from sin, we are offered mercy and grace from God; we are offered freedom and not death. But for Jesus Christ, He received the wrath of God in our place. He tore the veil of the temple granting us complete access to God. There is no more death for us, only life, and life everlasting. Matthew 27:51.

So, Esther was letting Mordecai know that it had been thirty days since the last time that she had been in the presence of the king. Not only that, but that if she does this, this would be a very big risk she was taking, it could be her life.

Verses 13- 14

And Mordecai told them to answer Esther: "Do not think in your heart that you will escape in the king's palace any more than all the other Jews.

For if you remain completely silent at this time, relief and deliverance will arise for the Jews from another place, but you and your father's house will perish. Ye who knows whether you have come to the kingdom for such a time as this."

They told Mordecai everything word for word that Esther had said to tell him. Every t crossed and every i dotted. Esther was in between a rock and hard place. So, Mordecai gives them his reply to Esther's command, that even though she is the queen and living inside the palace; that she is no safer than the Jews throughout the entire kingdom. She to was going to find herself in the firing line of being executed, because she to is a Jew.

He goes on to tell her that if she keeps silent about her people and her religion now. That their deliverance for their entire people would come from another direction or source. This book is silent on God, but I can't help to believe that Mordecai's thinking was just like Job's thinking. That although he had never seen Him, He knows his redeemer lives and will bring about deliverance to his people. I believe that he is looking back at the promises of God to Abraham. That his seed would become a great nation. That He, (God) would bless those who bless him and curse those who curse him. He recalls that the Messiah that God promised would come from his seed.

I believe that he remembered the stories told to him how God delivered them from Egyptian bondage. How He brought them through dry ground through the Red Sea. How God feed them and gave them water in the wilderness for forty years. He's a man of faith, he is trusting God. Maybe, just maybe he was thinking to himself and believing that the Messiah would come and deliver them Himself.

Then he goes on to say, "But thou and thy father's house will perish." I believe this statement he made is telling us, all the Bible gives no other details. That Esther possibly had brother and sisters. She could have been the youngest child, and that is why Mordecai adopted her as his own. They may have been older than her and probably had families of their own. So he is telling her that their entire family clan would be destroyed and wiped out. There would be no more trace of her family line.

Last of all. The entire book rest on what he stated next. "And who knows whether you have come to the kingdom for such a time as this." Although he does not mention God by name here, he is doing so between the lines. He is telling her that this may be the reason you were chosen to be queen. Although he is sitting in sackcloth and ashes, he sees the hand of God at work in the life of Esther.

This reminds me of the life of Jesus. How? Because when Jesus came to this earth, He came just at the right time when God had planned it. The nation of Israel was in great turmoil, being ruled by the Romans at the time. When He came into this world it was supernatural, through the work of the Holy Spirit; born of a virgin. God's way of doing things is far different than doing things our way. At first it doesn't make sense, but in the end we can see that it does.

God can use any of us, at any given time, for any situation, to bring about His purpose and plan. I believe that God moved to have this book put in His Holy Word for Israel as well as for the church. Because I believe this book points us towards future events. There will come a time of persecution for the church and Israel. There has always been a hatred toward both Israel and Christians. Although through the years there has been crusades to extinguish both, both Israel and the church are still thriving today.

Things just don't happen accidentally with God, they happened because that is how He planned it from the beginning of the world. I can look back across my early years in life, when I had near death experiences. Yes I was very close to deaths door. But God in His amazing Grace, stepped in, protected me and allowed me to live until this very day. I am so grateful to Him for this.

Listen to me and listen closely. You are not an accident my friend. I don't care who you are, where you come from, who your parents are. I don't care if they told you that you where an accident, you are not. God planned the very time of your life and when your life began. Sure you have made mistakes and sinned, but that isn't the end of your life, He has so much more to do in and through you. He is bringing you up, each step of the way, until He brings you to the point in your life as in Esther's life. Just trust Him. First accept Him into your life, by believing that Jesus is God's Son, that He died for your sins, was buried and arose from the dead to give you life and victory over sin. It's up to you now.

Do not misunderstand me. Being a Christian does not mean that you become rich on this earth with material things. He wants to make you rich spiritually, and that begins with a personal relationship with Him.

Verses 15-17

Then Esther told them to reply to Mordecai:

"Go gather all the Jews who are present in Shushan, and fast for me; neither eat nor drink for three days, night or day. My maids and I will fast likewise. And so I will go to the king, which is against the law; and if I perish, I perish!"

So Mordecai went his way and did according to all that Esther commanded him.

For one last time, Esther sent her messengers to Mordecai with a reply to help relieve him of his suffering and distress. We see from her words in verse sixteen that she is a wise and virtuous woman. She tell Mordecai to go and gather all the Jews in the city of Shushan together. Once he has done this he and all the Jews are to fast for her for three days. The number three conveys the meaning of completeness. It appears 467 times in God's Word. (From www.biblestudy.org) We have the Holy Trinity, God the Father, God the Son, and God the Holy Spirit. Jesus prayed three times in the garden before His arrest. Jesus was three days in the grave and arose again the third day. He used the example of Jonah being in the Great Fish to describe Him being in the grave three days.

So, for three days they were to fast, they were to go without food and drink for three days. So, all the Jews in Shushan including Esther and her seven maids was going to fast.

Jesus taught the disciples this in His sermon on the mount in Matthew 6:16-18:

> ***"And when you fast don't make it obvious as the hypocrites do for they try to look miserable and disheveled so people will admire them for their fasting. I tell you the truth that is the only reward they will ever get. But when you fast comb your hair and wash your face. Then no one will notice that you are fasting, except your Father who knows what you do in private. And your Father who sees everything will reward you." NLT.***

Fasting, which is linked to prayer is to be a private matter between us and God. We are not to parade around as Jesus said, "Like the Hypocrites," meaning the religious leaders of his day. Everything they did was for show, nothing pure from their hearts.

We have probably encountered people like this in our lifetime. They are walking around looking all sad, unshaved, uncombed hair, down hearted and pious. They look like they have heartburn from last night or they swallowed a peach seed. You ask them if everything is alright with them, then they brag about that they are fasting. Jesus said to be just the opposite from them. Take care of our personal hygiene, to wear a smile of joy on our face. God looks at the heart of us, not the natural appearance of doing things.

As I stated before fasting and praying are closely related to each other. So during this time I believe that they were also praying for Esther while they were also fasting for her. They were to be doing this for her because of what she said about going before the king without him asking for you.

Esther realized that this was bigger than she was as well as her people and that God was the only one who could bring about this deliverance of her people. She was seeking the face of God, before going in and facing the king.

If all of this does not work out, she tells Mordecai, "If I perish, I perish!" In other words, either way it goes, it is still God's will. She'll either die for breaking the law of the king by going to him unannounced or she will die by the plans that Haman has made. If so, so be it!

So far, I can see that Esther as well as Mordecai are inside the will of God. God has Esther right where He wants her and need her to be. I can see that once again that God is using a woman instead of a man for His plans. This

Book is named after Esther, the other Book of the Bible is named after a woman and that is Ruth.

I believe that God is telling us not to down upon women and mistreat them, because; after all He created them to for a purpose. He is using Esther not as a general of an Army to save His people, but as a gentle, humble, obedient wife and His servant.

I see her role her as the same role as Jesus. Jesus came humbly to this earth as God's obedient servant. She was the go between for her people to the king, and Jesus is our go between to the Father and us. She said, "If I perish, I perish!" Jesus said, "Not My will be done, but Your will done!" She was willing to perish for her people, Jesus laid down His life for the entire world.

I also see her as a future Israel, when God said that He would return them to their land and bless them again. He also said, "that they would be different from their ancestors. They had a heart of stone, (the Law), but He would give them a hear of flesh. Therefore, Israel would be more obedient towards Him and He would bless them.

Then I she here as a symbol of the Bride of Christ, the church. Willing and obedient to Him, faithful, compassionate and willing to die for Him, as He died for her.

To me Esther is a very amazing woman, being used by an Amazing God. She didn't panic, she was very level head, discerning, humble and wise. She also got Mordecai to get up and to get to work fasting for her; instead of sitting around in sackcloth and ashes all day.

J. Thomas Ruble II

5

Esther to the Rescue

Before moving on into chapter five of Esther I want to do a little recap, if you will. So far we have learned about King Ahasuerus who in history is known as Xerxes. We know that he is a very wealthy king, from the description given of his palace in Shushan. We also know that he is a king who likes to party, show off, brag and get drunk. We've also seen how he was very demanding for his queen, Queen Vashti to show off her beauty. But then we see that he is very hot tempered, which brought about his divorce from her. Next, we see that he's just not got a taste for the wine, but he has a lustful taste for women as well. And last of all he has a poor judgement in choosing his leaders under him. As we have seen him give a promotion to Haman which has lead to a law having them all killed.

Then we have learned about Mordecai and Esther. He is a godly man, who serves as one of the king's servants at his gate. He has raised his young cousin since she was very young and adopted her as his own. Then he sees the opportunity for her to become queen and enters her into the beauty pageant. He ends up saving the king's life by telling Esther about the plot of his murder by two of his closet servants. He is not rewarded for this service that he did for the king. But that he suffers and mourns for his people because of the law made to destroy his people. This came about because he would not bow down to Haman. He will only bow the knee to God as God told them in the Ten Commandments.

Last of all we've seen that Esther entered the beauty contest and won the favor of the king. She becomes queen and the king throws her a big bash for being the new elected queen. She finds out from Mordecai about the plot on the king's life and tells him about in the name of Mordecai. Then we see how calm she is from the last chapter of finding out the problem with Mordecai and coming up with a plan of fasting before going in to see him. She is a little apprehensive about going in before him unannounced because it could mean death for her. But she is a woman who will take it on the chin for her people.

Verses 1-2

Now it happened on the third day that Esther put on her royal robes and stood in the inner court of the king's palace, across from the king's house, while the king sat on his royal throne in the royal house, facing the entrance of the house.

So it was when the king saw Queen Esther standing in the court, that she found favor in his sight, and the king held out to Esther the golden scepter that was in his hand. Then Esther went near and touched the top of the scepter.

The third day had come, it was the very last day of the fasting of the Jews. Now the time had come, for Queen Esther to put off from fasting and for her to go in before the king. Once she ended the fasting process, she gets all gussied up for the king, by putting on her royal robes. What better way to get the king's attention by being all dressed up and looking good.

I believe it is good for a woman to dress up and to look nice for their husbands and no one else. I know that I love it when my bride of twenty-two years gets all dressed up for me. Women should take some pride in her appearance and dress up without being too revealing, showing everything. I mean come on who would want to come home every day to someone with, curlers in her hair, mud caked on her face, wearing ragged clothes, with big puff pink slippers. That is not attractive at all.

Several years ago, we went to the Titanic in Pigeon Forge, Tennessee; for a Valentines dinner. We had spent nearly two weeks finding a dinner dress for her. Then we spent two hours getting dressed up for the dinner. When I seen her in that dress we bought her, she was more beautiful than the day when we were married. I couldn't take my eyes off her, because she was so beautiful. And in my opinion, she was the most beautiful woman there at the dinner. Now it would have been a different story if she'd wore her everyday clothes to the dinner. I wouldn't have taken her to the dinner at all.

But now that Esther was all decked out in her royal clothes, the next step was the biggest one; going to present herself to the king. I can only image that she was very, very nervous about doing this, and it was very understanding why. Because if he did not find favor with her, she could be killed.

It has been a entire month since he had last seen Queen Esther. Maybe that was a good thing in her favor. Like they always say, "Absence makes the heart grow fonder." But as soon as he sees her, she found favor in his sight. I believe this old boy had finally found temperament in his life. I believe he had learned a lesson from the events that had transpired with Vashti. I also believe that Ahasuerus loved Esther very much as a husband should love his wife.

It must have been a great relief to Queen Esther when he held out that golden scepter to her. Because this is really what she was looking for and was hoping for. Once she seen him holding it out to her, she walked with more confidence towards him and touched the scepter.

So far everything is going just the way the Lord had planned it. The Lord already knew he wasn't going to kill her. She didn't know it but she was in the hands of the one who knew. I believe although the Bible doesn't tell us, I believe she was praying in her mind and under her breath.

Many times we ourselves see things happening to us as it is to Queen Esther here. Things look more like a towering mountain standing before us. To many times we wring our hands, fret and worry about little things like this. But make no mistake about it, God never sits in heaven on His throne, wring His hands. To many times we'll hee haw around with problems on our hearts, thinking they are to important for us to tell God about them.

Verses 3-5

And the king said to her, "What do you wish, Queen Esther? What is your request? It shall be given to you up to half the kingdom!"

So Esther answered, "If it pleases the king, let the king and Haman come today to the banquet that I have prepared for him."

Then the king said, "Bring Haman quickly, that he may do as Esther has said." So the king and Haman went to the banquet that Esther had prepared.

He must have known that something was going on with Queen Esther, and that something was bothering her. Because it had been some time since they had seen each other, and he did not request her presence. So he asked her two questions and made her an offer.

The first question was, "What is it you wish, Queen Esther?"

The second question, "What is your request?"

Whatever it was, "He would give it to her up to half his kingdom!"

This was a custom of theirs in the Orient. It was like giving them a blank check or better yet when we say, "The skies the limit!"

There was another time in the Bible when a man said this to another woman. It is found in Mark 6:23. It is the story of John the Baptizer and King Herod. King Herod had John put in prison because he had preached against King Herod for marrying his brother's wife. So King Herod had him thrown into prison for calling them adulterers.

But the day came on King Herod's birthday to be exact, that his wife's daughter danced for him. She had performed so well for him, that he said, "Ask me whatever you want, and I will give it to you. Whatever you ask me I will give you up to half my kingdom." So she ran and asked her mother what she should ask for, and she told her, for the head of John the Baptizer, on a silver platter.

But as for Queen Esther, she was not interested in receiving half the kingdom. She went straight to his heart, what does the king love more than anything, a good banquet. He loves to eat and drink if you ask me, so what better way to a mans heart than through his stomach.

Now this banquet is just not a banquet for the king, but it is for her enemy and her people's enemy. The Bible teaches us to this in several scriptures in the Bible:

Proverbs 25:21 If your enemies are hungry, give them food to eat. If they are thirsty, give them water to drink. NLT

Jesus taught this in His sermon on the mount, Matthew 5:43-45

"You have heard that it was said, You shall love your neighbor and hate your enemy. But I say to you, lover your enemies, bless those who curse you, do good to those who hate you and pray for those who spitefully use you and persecute you, that you may be sons of

5: Esther to the Rescue

your Father in heaven; for He makes the sun rise on the evil and on the good, and sends rain on the just and unjust." NKJV

Then again in Romans 12:20:

"Therefore if your enemy is hungry feed him; if he is thirsty give him a drink; for in so doing you will heap coals of fire on his head."

This is something that is not, and I mean is not an easy thing for us to do. It goes against human nature, because we always want to get back or get even with people. Most of the time when we want to give them something to eat, it is usually our fist we want to feed them. Believe me I know all to well from experiencing this in my lifetime.

It started when I was thirteen years old, when our family left our home church. The pastor at that time called our dad and another deacon into his pastor study at the church building after Sunday Services. When dad arrived to the car, we found out that the pastor had cussed him and the other deacon out. We learned what he had called them, and I was furious. I made a vow to fight anyone who called me that name, that he had called our dad. From that day on I kept that promise to my self, but it grew inside of me worse than a cancer. The longer I held to that grudge, other things got snagged on it, until I just became unbearable to live with. Believe you me, it drug me down until I hit rock bottom. Then I finally waved the white flag to the Lord and asked Him to help me with this. It's taken ten years to learn this lesson, and sometimes I fail at, repent, and move on. Doing it God's way, and the way that Esther is doing it, brings about a lot of peace of mind, and wasted energy. So I give it to Him and let him handle those who mistreat me, laugh at me, or persecute me. And last of all be nice to them and help them out when they need help. It works, it really works.

If you remember back in chapter one of Esther, that the men and women did not go to the same banquet together. Then they had another banquet when Esther became queen, and they probably dined separately.

But here in verse five, we see that the king waste no time, going to the banquet that Esther has prepared. Then he tells his servants to hurry up and get

Haman and for him to come at once to the banquet. As if Haman's head isn't already big enough, this will be the icing on the cake to inflate it even more.

Only thing is Haman doesn't know that Esther knows all about his evil plans to kill her people. He also doesn't know that she is a Jew and his plans includes killing her the queen. Also at this time the king is absolutely clueless that she is a Jew as well. And that Haman's plans include killing her.

King Ahasuerus loves banquets, and he reminds me of a old country song, *"I'm going to hire a wineo, to decorate our Home."* This song is about a woman who comes up with a plan, to decorate their home into a bar. This way, this will keep her man at home, and keep all his hard earn paycheck at home. That way the next morning while he's sleeping off his hangover, she is putting the money in the bank.

To me King Ahasuerus is a glutton and a winebibber. He's a married man, acting like he's got the entire world by the tail. He is always eating, drinking and making merry his heart with a spirit. He was just like a little kid in a candy store. Not only that, he is going to be putty in the hands of Esther.

Verses 6-8

At the banquet of wine the king said to Esther, "What is your petition? It shall be granted you. What is your request, up to half the kingdom? It shall be done!"

Then Esther answered and said, "My petition and request is this:

"If I have found favor in the sight of the king, and if it pleases the king to grant my petition and fulfill my request, then let the king and Haman come to the banquet which I will prepare for them, and tomorrow I will do as the king said."

I'd say that both the king and Haman are pretty much intoxicated from their drinking. I'd say that Haman's ego is living it up as well, being at a banquet with the king and queen. He's feeling pretty good about everything up to this point. He's prime minister of the kingdom, he's got a plan to exterminate the Jews, and now he is living it up with the king and queen.

As for Queen Esther, she is still filled with a little apprehension, about saying why she has prepared this banquet. Deep down she knows that this just

5: Esther to the Rescue

isn't the right time to make it known of what Haman is planning to do to her. She is also nervous about making it know to them that she is a Jewish woman.

Just then he ask her the same questions as he had previously asked her in verse three.

"What is your petition?"

"It shall be granted you."

"What is your request, up to half the kingdom?"

You know who he reminds me of? He reminds me of a car salesman! They will repeat and repeat the same line over and over to sell a car. It got me to thinking about there being something really bad about his kingdom. There's got to be something wrong with it because he is really trying to get rid of it.

Well, Esther's petition and request is this; if she has found favor in the eyes of the king, and if it pleases the king. I want you and Haman to come to another banquet that I am having tomorrow, and I will do as the king has said to me.

This probably wasn't the answer that the king was looking for, but it is her answer to his question. I'd say that she is waiting for the very right time, and right place to let it be known to the king. That is when she will make her identity known to the king and Haman.

But Esther is doing something here what we kids in the Eighty's would have said, "She's play it cool man!" She is wanting to know that the king really loves her and will not turn his back on her. She wants to know if he approves of her, and she has his total support. Because after all she probably knows why he had Vashti banished as queen, and she is testing the waters to see if he'll do the same to her. This little banquet today, is just an appetizer compared to what kind of shin dig she's going to have tomorrow. Little note: let's watch Haman's reaction to all of this up to this point. It's worth noticing.

Verses 9-10

So Haman went out that day joyful and with a glad heart; but when Haman saw Mordecai in the king's gate, and that he did not stand or tremble before him, he was filled with indignation against Mordecai.

Nevertheless Haman restrained himself and went home, and he sent and called for his friends and his wife Zeresh.

I told you to watch Haman's reaction didn't I. If his head swelled up anymore, he'd be a hot air balloon. His head is way beyond the clouds isn't it! He's on cloud nine, strutting his stuff.

Right now, he's thinking, "I've got it made. I just had lunch with the king and queen. Just little old me, and no one else, me, myself, and I." This is nothing more than pride on his part. This type of pride is different that us taking pride in our work we do. This type of pride is what God hates. This pride is what brought the downfall of Satan and the angels who followed him. Read Isaiah 14:12-15.

Proverbs 16:18 tells us, ***"Pride goeth before destruction and an haughty spirit before a fall."***

Jesus taught the disciples as well as us today in Matthew 23:12, ***"And whoever exalts himself will be humbled, and he who humbles himself will be exalted."***

There is a stark contrast difference between Mordecai and Haman, let me explain this. Back in Chapter two of Esther, Mordecai found out about the kings two doorkeepers were plotting to kill him, remember. Well, he told Queen Esther about it, who informed the king about it, who made an inquiry about the matter. When he learned that the information was true, he had them hung on the gallows.

Mordecai did not strut around like a little Banty Rooster, patting himself on the back, and announcing it to the entire city of Shushan; that he just saved the kings life. He didn't even get a thank you, nor did he even get rewarded for doing it. He simply faded back into everyday life sitting at the king's gate. But not Haman, he walked out of there joyful and with a glad heart. Head held high, strutting around, head in the clouds, proud, prideful admiring himself.

King Saul was a man of pride, 1 Samuel chapter 13- chapter 15. He offered a sacrifice that he was not supposed to offer, only Samuel was. Samuel told him to wait for him, but when Samuel didn't show Saul made the sacrifice. Then he made a rash vow to his men that anyone who ate anything would be killed that day. His son Jonathan did not hear the vow because he and his armor bearer were fighting the Philistines. They came to the place where honey was lying on the ground and Jonathan ate some. Well Saul finds out about it and comes close of killing his own son, but the people saved him. Then last of all in Chapter 15 we read that God gave Saul the command of killing all the

Amalekites and everything they own. But he spared their king Agag, as well as the sheep and oxen. That's when Samuel told Saul that God had rejected him as king of Israel because of his pride and disobedience.

King Nebuchadnezzar was another king who was filled with pride. We read about what happened to him in Daniel chapter four.

He had a dream of a great tree. Daniel was the only one who could explain the meaning of the dream to him. Come to find out the tree in the dream was Nebuchadnezzar himself. After Daniel explained the meaning to him, Daniel pleaded whole heartily with him to stop sinning and to do what was right. But he didn't listen and kept on sinning against God. His pride got the best of him, he began saying, "Look what I did! Look what I built! I,I,I.

The next thing he knew, he went insane. He slept in the wild, his hair and nails grew long, he ate grass like an ox. He recovered from this madness because he looked up to heaven and acknowledged God and his sins. He began to praise and worship God, and God gave him back his throne.

Today we have a group of people who call themselves pride. Don't forget my friends what God's word says, "Pride goes before destruction and a haughty spirit before a fall." I realize that we live in the year of 2022, but God is still God, and He is the same Yesterday, Today, and Forever, Hebrews 13:8. I pray that you come to the Lord before you die or before He returns. Because if not there is destruction and judgment coming.

Notice also that his pride has indignation towards Mordecai, because he will not bow down to him. He resents Mordecai and what he stands for and will not bow to him. Do they not also do this to us today as the church. They say that they are all about love and transparency but are they really. No, not really. Oh, they are if we agree with them and what they are doing is right. But if we take a stand against it, then we are bigots, hateful, full of hate, and not for love and acceptant. They hurl hateful words our way as if firing a fully loaded M16, towards us. Taking people to court because they don't accept them as couples and will not bake a cake for their wedding. If that's the case take your business to someone who will bake your cake for your wedding. Your pride and arrogance is destroying people's lives and their livelihood.

Verses 10-14

Nevertheless Haman restrained himself and went home, and he sent and called for his friends and his wife Zeresh.

Then Haman told them of his great riches, the multitude of his children, everything in which the kind had promoted him, and how he had advanced him above the officials and servants of the king.

Moreover Haman said, "Besides Queen Esther invited no one but me to come in with the king to the banquet that she prepared; and tomorrow I am again invited by her, along with the king."

"Yet all this avails me nothing, so long as I see Mordecai the Jew sitting at the king's gate."

Then his wife Zeresh and all his friends said to him, "Let a gallows be made, fifty cubits high, and in the morning suggest to the king that Mordecai be hanged on it; then go merrily with the king to the banquet." And the thing pleased Haman; so he had the gallows made.

Let's not pass up the word Nevertheless. It's meaning is: in spite of that. It would be like us using the word however today when telling a story to people.

Then the next word to look at is the word refrained, which means: To keep oneself from doing, feeling or indulging in something and especially from following a passing impulse.

What this is telling us here is it is pointing back to his reaction towards Mordecai in the last verse. Remember he had indignation or in other words deep seceded anger of laying hands on him. But instead of going off on impulse and doing it, he let it go. Why is that?

The first reason is because his pride and ego is inflated from having lunch with the king and queen. Second, he knows that the fate of Mordecai and all the Jews and the great slaughter day is coming for them. He wasn't going to allow Mordecai to rain on his self indulging, prideful parade.

Using restraint is not a sign of weakness. To often we've been duped by movies as well as society not to show restraint; and to just tear into people. This lesson has been a school of hard knocks for myself. You can ask just about anyone who knows me, that I just did not use restraint. I just could not let something be, I would have to tell the person off, get in the last word, throw a punch or seek revenge on people. That my friends is what we call sin! This sin is one that reside in all of us, saved or unsaved. We write it off and call it "HUMAN NATURE" today. God calls it sin.

I'm not saying that I have perfected it, all I know is that the Lord Himself has had to work overtime on me to let it go. To forgive the person(s), to love them, and to pray for them. If I had learned this lesson when I was younger, it would have saved me a lot of unwanted grief.

Jesus spoke about this in His Sermon on the Mount, Matthew 5:9-12, 38-48. He told us to rejoice when persecuted, to be a peace maker, to love our enemies, when and if they cause; physical or mental harm to us. This goes against our very nature. He is wanting us to be just like God the Father, as well as Himself. Although Jesus was very much God, He was very much human. He had all the same feelings and desires we had, except He never sinned. He resisted sin and the sinful desires of the flesh, but He overcame. We know that He overcame because He never once retaliated against those who insulted Him, threatened Him, or lied about Him, 1 Peter 2:23.

Haman here just brushes it off because like I said, "He isn't going to allow this man to rain on his parade. In doing so his pride now has the better of Him. Now he is bragging. He sends messages to his friends, his wife and his children to gather around him; so he can gloat about the things that has happened to him. He want's to toot his little horn loudly.

It must have been some time since he had been home. The reason I say that is because he brags about the riches the king has given him, the promotion he had received from the king. Not only that but that how he was promoted above all the princes and servants that the king had.

Haman sounds just like his father the devil. He was second highest man in the kingdom. The devil prided himself by saying that he would rise above God and ascend to His throne. He bragged about but ended up being cast out of heaven. But his bragging has just begun. He isn't through with it, he's going to put the icing on the cake.

He tops off his own cake, with the most perfect icing, that he had just had lunch with the king and queen. And, to top that off, the queen, has invited me to another banquet tomorrow, just me, nobody else.

He really thinks he's something and someone now, that he has had lunch with them and is attending tomorrow. Only thing is he thinks that this banquet is in his honor, but it is really Esther's way of exploiting his plans of killing her and her people the Jews. This man doesn't realize that he's holding his own knife to his throat and committing suicide.

The Word of God has one word name for a man like Haman. That name is FOOL! We can learn a valuable lesson from the parable that Jesus taught in Luke 12:16-21.

This parable is about a rich farmer. He had a farm with very rich soil, that brought in a crop of all crops. It would have been a crop that we would have longed for on the farm.

Instead of giving God the glory for the fertile ground, sunshine, the rain, and for the abundant crop. He said he did not have enough barns to put his crops in. So he tore down barns to build bigger barns to put his crops in. But then he'd lay back and take it easy, because he is now on easy street. But God called him a Fool! He died and didn't get to enjoy easy street. Jesus went on to say that this life isn't about storing up treasure's here on this earth. It here today and gone tomorrow. I coined a phrase that goes like this, "What took years to build, took only seconds to be destroyed." It's true. We do not know what tomorrow holds, and all the things that we have will someday belong to someone else.

Haman is like this rich farmer. He is a fool! He like the rich farmer thinks we've got it made and on easy street. But always remember this, easy street also has potholes, detours and dead ends as well.

Next thing we see about Haman is this. He has moved on from bragging to sniveling. He is just like a little undisciplined, spoiled brat kid. He has been chosen by the king to be prime minister of his kingdom, second in command to the king. He has power and authority, only the king has more than he has. But here in verse thirteen he is worrying about Mordecai not bowing down to him. So what! Get over it Haman, stop worrying about that and do your job.

Everyone of us has at some time in our lives run in to this situation and have probably acted like him. We want respect, we want to be loved, liked, and accepted by others. But instead of moving on, we'll mope around because of one person who will not respect us. Little things like this can destroy us

5: Esther to the Rescue

personally. Little things like this is destroying our cities, our towns, our communities, our states and our nation.

No one! And I mean NO ONE, living before us as well as today, has suffered anymore than what the Lord Jesus Christ suffered. He suffered more than anyone, has that has ever lived. Think about. He was criticized for healing on the Sabbath, opening blind eyes, casting out demons, called the devil, illegitimate, betrayed by Judas and abandoned by the others.

He was called a drunk, a glutton, Peter denied Him, He was falsely accused, beat almost to death, laughed at, mocked, stripped naked and put on the cross, given poison to drink, crucified between to thieves. He never once complained about the injustice done to Him, as a matter of fact, he said, "Father forgive them, for they know not what they do."

It just wasn't the people of His day that done this to Him. Because He died for the entire world to be saved, so it was you and I that did it to Him as well. There are still some today that is making fun of Him in bad jokes or saying that He sinned when He didn't. Some say that He was married, or that He was gay, but He was not. He was and still is the Son of God, who died for our sins, to provide a way for us to God, and is one day returning to this world to set everything in order.

Haman is a little man, with a big ego, and holding a very important job. I can't help but think that he is not the right man for being Prime Minister of Persia. Because if a little thing like this gets him upset, something bigger than this will crush him.

Last of all to close out this chapter, we see that Haman's wife Zeresh whose name means "gold" (Smith's Bible Dictionary). As well as all of his friends, give him bad advice in building a gallows for hanging Mordecai on. This gallows is a frame usually of two upright post and a transverse beam from which criminals are hanged on. (Webster's Dictionary). This gallows was to be fifty cubits high. A cubit was a ancient unit of measurement. It was from the tip of the middle finger to the elbow and was about eighteen inches. (Webster's Dictionary).

This would be 50X18= 900 divided by 12 = 75 feet tall. So this gallows was going to be seventy five feet tall. This to me is an over kill making something this tall to hang someone on. But after all, he just didn't want to kill, Mordecai, he wanted to humiliate him as well. This would have sent a message to everyone in the kingdom, this is what happens for not giving honor to Haman.

Once he had the gallows built for his enemy Mordecai, he was to speak to the king about having Mordecai killed on the gallows. This way one man would die for all instead of everyone being killed. More less, chop the head off the snake and the rest will die. This way he could go into the banquet a very happy and cheerful man; know the king would go along with his plan of killing Mordecai.

"Oh, what a tangled web we weave, when first we practice to deceive." (Sir Walter Scott).

We must be very careful seeking the advice of wicked poor, counselors. Because evil schemes like this are ill-advised and dangerous. They can end up being of our own undoing. In other words, we can catch our own britches with our own pitchfork.

This plan of his wife and friends made him very happy though, I can only image that he was chomping at the bit to tell the king about it. So, he wasted no time in having the gallows to be built that day.

Maybe you've been here in a situation like Mordecai. Someone isn't plotting your death, but they are plotting against you, without you even knowing about it. It may not kill you physically, but it would have lasting effects on you spiritually and emotionally. In a way it is called persecution and murder on your character. Well let me say when this happens we are not alone. Because our Lord Jesus suffered the same things. But He has given us words to lift us up and encourage us.

John 15:18 "If the world hates you, remember that it hated Me first."

Before Jesus came into the world he created, while still in the womb of Mary. There was no place in the inn for Him and his earthly family. He was born into this world in a damp, smelly cave used as a stable. He did not have a comfortable baby bed. His bed was a manger.

In Luke 4:16-30 Jesus stood up and read the book of Isaiah 61:1-2 in thee synagogue in His hometown of Nazareth. After reading this He tells those gathered there that He Himself has fulfilled this prophecy. Well, needless to say that didn't go over well with them. So they run Him out towards a cliff in the city to throw Him off. But He knew this was not the way for Him to die, so He walked right down the middle of them.

I can see how this verse relates to what would happen to Jesus in the future. I can see how this relates to the Jews in the future. And I can also see how this relates to the church. We take a stand against sin, sinful things and wickedness. But God is standing in the Shadows watching over His people. We can't see Him or feel Him, but He is there. He knows all, and He sees all. He sees and knows their trappings for us, but Jesus said, and I believe it, "The gates of Hell will not prevail against it."

Mordecai is a type of Christ. He is a man full of sorrow, a man who is hated, and a man who is resented and plotted against. Both of their stories continue on.

J. Thomas Ruble II

6

God Reveals His Plan with a Sense of Humor

Verses 1-3

That night the king could not sleep. So one was commanded to bring the book of the records of the chronicles; and they were read before the king.

And it was found written that Mordecai had told of Bigthana and Teresh, two of the king's eunuchs, the doorkeepers who had sought to lay hands on King Ahasuerus.

Then the king said, "What honor or dignity has been bestowed on Mordecai for this?" and the king's servants who attended him said, "Nothing has been done for him."

As I have stated before, the Book of Esther does not mention the name of God. But we can see through these first six chapters, His name is not mentioned, but His fingerprints are all over these scriptures. Just because His name isn't mentioned does not mean that God is not at work in the lives of His people, or the entire world for that matter.

We can see His loving and caring hands are working for His people the Jews, namely Mordecai and Esther. We know this because Mordecai reported that two men who were the king's doorkeeper were plotting to kill the king. When it was found to be true, they were hanged, and it was written in the book of the chronicles of the Meds and Persian's.

But notice here that God's word tells us that the king couldn't sleep. This was not by happenstance, this is God working through His providence. He planned this, as well as placing insomnia upon the king. When God wants to put a man to sleep, He can and will do it. If He wants a man to be restless and have insomnia, He can and will do it.

In Genesis 2:21 NKJV:

And the Lord God caused a deep sleep to fall on Adam, and he slept; and He took one of his ribs, and closed up the flesh in its place.

This verse is really self explanatory. It really doesn't need to be interpreted. Its as plan as the nose on your face. God caused a deep sleep to fall on Adam. He underwent the anesthesia of God without the gases we use in operations. God put him to sleep to remove a rib from him, without pain, and without any scar. This tells us that we are ever so weak before an almighty God. And notice that God did this in a loving and caring way not to hurt Adam. God never ever intends to hurt or harm us, He is ever so loving and caring.

But when God wants a man to be wide awake, He will cause a restlessness within him. God did the same thing to Nebuchadnezzar, when he gave him a bad dream and he couldn't get back to sleep. We find this story in Daniel 2:1 and also in Daniel 6:18.

Since he couldn't get to sleep, he had them bring the Book of the Chronicles to read it to him. This would have been like a history book of past history written down. Just like the two Books 1 and 2 Chronicles in our Bibles is a history of the kings of Israel and Judah. To some people a history book being read to them is enough to put them to sleep.

But this wasn't by chance to where they had opened this book and began to read it to the king. This was the finger of God moving it right were He wanted them to open it and to begin to read it. So, they began to read it to the king.

In the Pulpit Commentary it was brought up to why the king himself did not read it; instead of having it read to him? Could it have been that the king could not read? Or was it the sound of someone else reading that soothed him and made him sleepy? Could have been either way I guess. But raised a good question for further study. However, I can remember the days when dad would read the Bible to us and pray before bedtime. Then once we were in bed, mom would read a Bible Story book or some other book to us. I can still hear her sweet, soft voice reading those stories at almost a whisper. Even when it came to an exciting part to where those in the story raised their voices, her voice was still at a whisper but at a little higher pitch. She did that to make it more soothing to us, to calm us down to be able to sleep better.

As for myself, reading the Bible or history to me at night gets me worked up and can't sleep. I love to read both and to watch it on the History Channel. I believe that King Ahasuerus loved to hear it read to him for several reasons, 1) I believe that it gave him a sense of accomplishment, of the things that he had accomplished in his reign as king. 2) I believe he had it read to him to find out about any loose ends that may have been undone. 3) I believe he had it read to him often about past failures of what not to do again. Something that we fail to do today. 4) I do not believe that he was illiterate. I believe that he loved to hear someone read it who was a good reader and had soothing voice to help calm him down.

Remember that this event read to him in verses two and three, took place in chapter 2:21-23. Mordecai had overheard these two men plotting to kill the king. He told Queen Esther about the plot, who then told the king about it. When they investigated into the plot and found it to be true; Bigthana and Tresh were killed for plotting to murder the king.

More times than not, those closet to us are the one's to watch out for, they can be our worst enemies. King David before he became King of Israel was Saul's bodyguard and played the harp for him. But King Saul had a jealous eye for David and tried twice to kill him with a spear, then chased him down for years to kill him.

Judas Iscariot was one of the twelve disciples, even the treasure of the group. We all know that he stole from them, (John 12:6) and he betrayed Jesus for thirty pieces of silver. But then eventually went out and killed himself for betraying Jesus.

Now what Mordecai had done for the king was written down in the annuals of history. The king owed everything to Mordecai for saving his life. If Mordecai had not told Queen Esther about the plot, then they would have killed the king. However, I believe he was about to doze off to sleep when he heard this read, then all at once his ears perked up. He raised himself up in bed and asked, "What has been done to show this man Mordecai respect and reward?"

So, his servants looked at the book again and said, "Nothing!" All that was written is that Mordecai told us about the plot and those trying to kill you, but he was never rewarded for saving your life."

Sometimes God will allow things to be overlooked like this and go unrewarded for a time. Sometimes God will allow us to be rewarded for the things that we have done at once. But often time, the greatest blessing and reward is those times when we are rewarded later. Just as R.G. Lee preached, "Pay Day, Someday." There is a day coming when ALL of us will be rewarded for the things that we have done for the Lord Jesus Christ.

Jesus said in Matthew 6:19-21 NLT:

Don't store up treasures here on earth, where moth eat them and rust destroys them and where thieves break in and steal. Store up your treasures in heaven where moths and rust cannot destroy and thieves do not break in and steal. Wherever your treasure is there the desires of your heart will also be."

Everything here on this earth is going to rust, fade, rot, stolen and be destroyed, because we live in a fallen world. But the things that we store up in heaven can't no one or anything can touch them at all, because heaven is perfect, because God and Christ are perfect. No one can even break in there, because it is unreachable with a human body. I believe that God had left this undone, just for this moment and for this time.

All of us who are farmers know of this reward. When we began sowing the seeds of our crops. We had to work through the, fight through cool days, hot days, extremely hot days. Then we had to fight through no rain, a little rain, to much rain, strong winds, tornados blowing the crop over, to hail beating it to a pulp.

We had to chop out the weeds, plow and cultivate, side dress in the heat. The same held true when it came time to harvest the tobacco into the barn. Then we had to trudge through the cold and snow to pull leaves off the stalk and bale them. Then after weeks of pulling off the leaves and baling them it was time to take it to the market to sell. Once we seen that check, it felt like we were millionaires for all that hard labor. We had worked ten to eleven months out of that year to get paid, in order to pay bills, get new clothes, new shoes, food on the table. The best of all was when day would take us all out to eat as a family. What a treat this was, because we didn't have the money to eat out at restaurants but a few times through the year. Then came Christmas time and mom and dad gave of their hearts for us to have the best Christmas ever. We didn't get expensive gifts like some of our classmates, but what we got was love and something money couldn't buy.

Verses 4-6

So the king said, "Who is in the court?" Now Haman had just entered the outer court of the king's palace to suggest that the king hang Mordecai on the gallows that he had prepared for him."

The kings servants said to him, "Haman is there, standing in the court." And the king said, "Let him come in."

So Haman came in, and the king asked him, "What shall be done for the man whom the king delights to honor?" Now Haman thought in his heart, "Whom would the king delight to honor more than me?"

The king finally wanted to reward Mordecai for saving his life. So he asked his servants who was in the court? The king must have known there were servants in the court this time of the morning. He probably also heard them talking among themselves. But notice here that Haman had just arrived in the court, just as the king asked this question.

Now Haman's reason for being there and the reason for the king calling him was totally opposite of each other. The king was wanting to reward Mordecai, Haman was there to ask permission of the king to kill Mordecai. Haman has no idea that the king had the records of history read to him, and wanted to reward Mordecai.

So, Haman comes in to where the king is. Before he had time to make his request known to the king; the king ask him, "What shall be done unto the man whom the king delighted to honor?" Since Haman was his Prime Minister, he was looking to him for wisdom on the matter, of how to honor the man. But Haman was thinking about himself here, he is Prime Minister, wearing his signet ring, had been to a banquet given by the queen, and about to attend another one. Everything with Haman is, I,I,I and me, me, me. But what he doesn't realize is his bubble is about to be popped, he's about to be eating crow. He is getting ready to eat part of God's Humble Pie.

The Bible tells us in Philippians:

Philippians 2:3 NLT "Don't be selfish; don't try to impress others. Be humble thinking of others as better than yourselves."

What Haman is proving here is to how the world operates. Selfishness, greed, and pride. This attitude or be-attitude does not and should not reflect the life of a Christian. But from time to time it will rear it's ugly face in our lives and our walk with the Lord. If and when it does we need to do as Barney Fife says, "Nip it! Nip it in the bud!" If we don't the Lord has His way of disciplining us, to make us humble; in order to have a right relationship with Him as well as with others.

Jesus is our example of ow to live this life while He lived upon the earth. On the night of His last hours of His life left here He humbled Himself before His disciples. He took off His outer garment, tied a towel around His waist, and made Himself a slave before them. He knelt down at their feet and washed their dirty, grimy feet.

In today's world it is totally opposite of being like Christ. It's a dog eat dog world, of want to be, got be number one, to be on top. People like this will do anything and everything, to others in order to reach that brass ring. Don't believe me! Take a good look around you when election times rolls around, look at the people who play sports. But make no mistake about it, everyone of us is guilt of being like Haman. The reason being is because of the old sin nature that lies within each and every person.

So, Haman is thinking about himself and how he should be rewarded, not another person.

Verses 7-9

And Haman answered the king, "For the man whom the king delights to honor,

6: God Reveals His Plan with a Sense of Humor

"Let a royal robe be brought which the king has worn, and a horse on which the king has ridden, which has a royal crest placed on its head.

"Then let this robe and horse be delivered to the hand of one of the king's most noble princes, that he may array the man whom the king delights to honor. Then parade him on horseback through the city square, and proclaim before him; 'Thus shall it be done to the man whom the king delights to honor!"

As I stated before, Haman is thinking about himself, in how he should be honored by the king. I believe that he was thinking that this would now be the time when Mordecai would finally bow before him. He has an evil heart as well as a evil eye. He is thinking, I am second in command to the king but how I would love to be in the king's palace on the throne. Then I would have power like the king and then earn the respect that went along with it. This would then, Mordecai would have no choice but to bow down to me, dressed like a king, honored as a king, and riding the kings horse that he rode.

Haman was wanting all the pomp and circumstance that went with being king of Persia. Oh king, place a royal robe that you wore up the man, (me). A horse that you have ridden upon, (me). And the royal crown that you wear, (me). He is wanting to look impressive, be impressive and to have the world know how impressive he really was. Not only that but to have someone to announce his honor and arrival made known while being lead on horseback. This is what is done by the king, to the man he is very well pleased in.

What a stark contrast between Jesus, Joseph and Daniel compared to Haman. Jesus, while being tempted by the devil, was taken up on high mountain and the devil showed Him all the kingdoms of the world and their glory. He told Jesus that He would give all of them to Him if He'd fall down and worship him. Jesus had none of that and told him, "Away with you Satan! For it is written 'You shall worship the Lord your God, and Him only you shall serve."

In John 6:1-15, was another time when the people wanted to make Jesus their King because of the miracle of the loaves and fishes. Jesus knew what was in their hearts and that they wanted to take Him by force, He departed again into the mountain by Himself. He did it God's way, by going to His death on a rugged cross, to become our sacrifice, Lord, Savior and King. One day, EVERY knee will bow before Jesus Christ. Everyone!

Joseph was taken out of prison to interpret Pharaoh's dreams. After doing so he told Pharaoh to find a wise man to be over the land of Egypt; in order to store up grain from the seven good years of crops. Joseph did not have himself in mind for this promotion, but God did. God Himself had Pharaoh bring this great promotion upon him. This was God's way of rewarding Joseph for his faithfulness to Him.

Pharaoh made Joseph second in command. He knew that God was with him and given him his great wisdom. He placed royal garments upon him, gave him a wife and had him ride in a chariot just for him. Everywhere he went people bowed down to him.

Daniel to was a man who was humble. King Nebuchadnezzar promoted him in chapter two of Daniel. He did this because he had interpreted the king's dream without even being told what the dream was. Then again in Daniel chapter five he tells King Belshazzar the writing on the wall. Belshazzar had told him if he would tell him the meaning of the writing, he'd reward him. But Daniel did not want anything from the king for the interpretation. But before Belshazzar died by the hand of the Persian Army, he rewarded him.

So, the king is going to take what Haman had suggested to him, and reward Mordecai with his own thoughts and words. This makes me chuckle and laugh. Yes, I find humor in this. God has his way of turning things on their heads to bring about His will. I see that God has a sense of humor. How? Well, He is going to take what Haman suggested to reward Mordecai, and Haman is going to lead this one-man parade of honor.

Verse 10

Then the king said to Haman, "Hurry, take the robe and the horse, as you have suggested, and do so for Mordecai the Jew who sits within the king's gate! Leave nothing undone of all that you have spoken."

Like I said, each time I read this, I read it with a smile and laugh. I can just picture the look on old Haman's face, standing there. His head is swelled up like a blistered garden hose, chest puffed out, with a big smile on his face; as the king begins to speak. He is thinking, oh yes Haman old man, here it comes.

King: Hurry. That means make haste, don't wait, do it now. Or as we were told in the military, "You should have done that yesterday."

Haman: Thinking to himself, yes, yes!

King: And the apparel

Haman: Yes, yes, yes!

King: And the horse as you have said.

Haman: Yes, yes, yes! Here it comes Haman, here it comes! This is the moment you've been waiting for. He's going to mention your name, because you deserve this great honor.

King: And do even so to

Haman: Oh boy, here it comes!

King: Mordecai the Jew that sits at the king's gate.

Haman: WHAT? Wait a cotton-picking minute here? Do What? Come again?

MORDECAI? Are you serious! Me! The Prime Minister go to this man I hate, ad despise and loath. You've got to be kidding me.

If Haman wore denture's back then in his day, they would have fallen out and hit the floor. He wasn't standing ten foot tall now, he was feeling about the size of a pea. What I wouldn't have given to be a fly on the wall to have seen the look on his face; the look of shock and awe. Then the look of bewilderment. Last the look of seething with anger. There would have been smoke coming out of his ears.

I don't care who you are, this is great. Like I said before, God has a sense of humor. God is like, so you hate Mordecai do you, you want to kill him today as well as all the Jews together. Well instead of killing him today you are going to honor him. I love it.

There was no waiting around to have this done, it had gone undone for to long now. The king was wanting this to be done, ASAP! AT ONCE! There was to be no delays in doing what Haman had been told to do by the king. So, Haman's hands were tied. There was nothing that he could do to get out of doing what the king requested. If he had argued about it, he would have lost his position as Prime Minister by being killed at the king's word.

Maybe you been overlooked, despised by Haman, and haven't been rewarded. Make no mistake about it, God has not forgotten you. If you think that He has please remember our Lord. Jesus spoke of Himself in Matthew 21:42 of the rejected stone. He was quoting from Psalm 118:22-23. He had come to His own people but those of the religious leaders rejected Him as God's Son, the Messiah. Jesus knows what it is like to be despised, rejected and overlooked.

There are times in our walk with the Lord when those around us; family, friends, co-workers and sometimes at church will reject us and overlook us. There will be a lot of faithful men and women alike who have faithfully served the Lord everyday, and often overlooked by others, but not overlooked by the Lord.

Verse 11

So Haman took the robe and the horse, arrayed Mordecai and led him on horseback through the city square, and proclaimed before him, "Thus shall be done to the man whom the king delights to honor!"

Haman had planned on getting the king's approval to kill Mordecai on this day. He had thought of leading him to his death on the gallows, but God stepped in. So instead of killing him he was dressed him in the king's apparel and leading him on horseback. As they went through the city square, he proclaimed a loud, "This is how the king honors the man whom he finds favor in.

Can you imagine the disappointment and the humiliation that Haman was experiencing. Here he was leading the man whom he hated, he despised and wanted to kill; for not bowing down to him. Instead of him getting this honor, he is being humiliated. His pride has gotten the best of him, leaving him to spiral downward. Remember I quoted Proverbs 16:18 about Pride goeth before destruction, and a haughty spirit before a fall. Well, this is just the beginning of his downfall, and the Word of God is never wrong.

Jesus spoke about this in Matthew 23:12;

"And whoever exalts himself will be humbled and he who humbles himself will be exalted.

Jesus was speaking about the religious leaders of his day, of how they dressed in great pomp, and acted all pious. But we see here that the same thing is very true of what is taking place with Mordecai and Haman.

Mordecai had humbled himself, by dressing in sackcloth and ashes for the law against killing the Jews. He sat at the king's gate, instead of acting like he was the best thing since goats milk. Haman on the other hand exalts himself, parades around like he's the best thing that has happened to Shushan.

Haman left nothing undone of how the king had told Haman to perform this honor for Mordecai. He placed the king's clothes on him, set him on the king's horse and lead him around. For a moment Mordecai was living the life of a king. I can only imagine that some people in the city square knew Mordecai and was doing a double take, saying to one another, "Why, that's Mordecai?" Some of them probably was wondering what had taken place for Mordecai to receive this honor.

I remember hearing B.R. Lakin saying one time in a sermon, "Dead noses smell no roses! We should honor and love another while we are living, and not to honor them after they die." There is a lot of truth in what he said. In fact, the Bible teaches us on several occasions to do just that.

The night that Jesus washed the disciple's feet, He told us to wash each other's feet. Myself I don't believe that He meant to literally wash the feet, but to humble ourselves before one another, and to help one another, giving honor to one another. Because looking the other way while a sister or brother in Christ is in need is a sin. Paul said the same thing in the book of Philippians.

Philippians 2:3 "Don't be selfish; don't live to make a good impression on others. Be humble, thinking oof others as better than yourself." TLB.

Its sad to say as well as to see that a whole lot of the world has found its way into the church today. People want to point the finger of blame at others for things that happened a hundred years ago, fifty years ago, ten years ago. There has been a lot of churches split because we as Christians will not humble ourselves and think that others are more important than ourselves. There are also a lot of people in the church today who feel they are more important because they are more educated, have more money, have more expensive homes than some within the church. Its sad to see and sad to hear of this.

Jesus had this type of spirit well up within the group of his disciples. It is found in Matthew 20:20-28 and Mark 10:35-45. In the account of Matthew, James and Johns mother came to Jesus with her sons and knelt down to make a request of Jesus. Jesus asked her, "What do you want?" She answered Him, "That He would grant her request that her two sons, that one would sit at His right hand and the other on his left hand in His kingdom.

Jesus told her and her sons that "You do not know what you are asking." Then He asked them a question, "Can you drink the cup I am going to drink?" They answered Him, "We can." He told them that they would drink the His cup. But to set on either side of Him was not His to grant. These seats belong to those who God has prepared them for.

Then notice what happened next in verse twenty-four. The other ten disciples heard this and boy were they mad. The bible used the word indignant. This means that they were angry and annoyed with James and John.

So to put out these flames of fires that had whooshed up between them. Jesus called them to Himself and told them that they know that the rulers of Gentiles lord it over them, and those who are great exercise authority over them. He goes on to tell them that this should be among them. For whoever desires to become great among you, let him be your servant. Whoever desires to be first among you, let him be your slave- Just as the Son of Man did not come to be served, but to serve and to give His life a ransom for many.

Jesus said, "Just as the Son of Man did not come to be served." He was talking about Himself here. He came into this world as a baby, born in a stable, and had a manger as a bed. He left ALL the splendor of heaven to come here and to live as one of us. He gave up a lot. "But to serve and to give his life a ransom for many." He came here to serve the people of His day and He serves us today. He washed our feet just as He washed the disciple's feet. But the greatest part of His servanthood came the day when He suffered a criminal's death, stripped naked and nailed to a wooden cross. He did this for us.

God takes care of His own. Instead of our enemies having honor over us, He grants us honor. Like I've stated before. He will have it done while we are still living, it may be five years, ten years or twenty years, but He will bring it about. Or He may simply wait and bestow that honor on us when we get home to heaven one day. However, He will prepare a table before us in the presence of our enemies, anoint our head with oil and make our cup to run over.

6: God Reveals His Plan with a Sense of Humor

Verses 12-14

Afterward Mordecai went back to the king's gate. But Haman hurried to his house, mourning and with his head covered.

When Haman told his wife Zeresh and all his friends everything that had happened to him, his wise men and his wife Zeresh said to him, "If Mordecai, before whom you have begun to fall, is of Jewish descent, you will not prevail against him but will surely fall before him."

While they were still talking with him the king's eunuchs came, and hastened to bring Haman to the banquet which Esther had prepared.

When Haman had finished the one-man parade with Mordecai. Mordecai goes right back to his job at the king's gate. He does not go around bragging about the great honor the king had rewarded him with. He simply returns to his job.

This reminds me of the time when Samuel had anointed David to be the King of Israel. Samuel anointed him when God told him to. But after Samuel had anointed him, David did not go straight to the king's palace and set down on the throne. He went back to his job of shepherding his father's sheep.

But for Haman he was embarrassed. Notice it says He hurried to his house. Of course, he was hurrying home, he was embarrassed, and needed a shoulder to whimper and cry on. He was getting out of dodge before someone recognized him and stopped him. Then notice it says that he was mourning and with his head covered. He is more than embarrassed now, he's crying because he has been humiliated. He did not want anyone to see him so he covered his head, he is ashamed to show his face in public. Because he is the Prime minister of Persia, and this wasn't a job for someone in his position. Oh, how the mighty have fallen.

So I believe he didn't just walk home on a nice little stroll, he was running as fast and hard as he could run to get away. He needed the love and support of his wife and his friends. He needed to be around people who would sympathize with him; as he whined, sulked and complained.

But notice that once he arrives home and tells them what had happened to him, it gets worse. Instead of giving him words to comfort him, they tell him what he didn't want to hear. That was the man Mordecai who is a Jewish man, more less you don't have a leg to stand on. In fact you have only begun to fall, you will not win over him and you will fall and be defeated before him.

Let me be frank and clear about something here. God gave Abraham a promise to make his seed into a great nation. He promised to bless those who blessed them and to curse those who curse them. I do not care what men or women say today about the Jews and that God is finished with them. Balderdash! God has not and will not give up on the Jews, He is not finished with them. In fact He is still blessing them today. Do they do everything right? No. Are they without sin? No. Neither are we, but God hasn't given up on us either.

For those who fight against them today mostly within their nation, you are fighting an exhaustive battle. You are not just fighting against Israel; you are fighting against the Lord; which is very dangerous. You are mad an anger with God, more than you are with Israel, because God gave His Prophetic Word to Isaiah:

Isaiah 66:8 "Who has heard or seen anything as strange as this? For in one day, suddenly, a nation, Israel shall be born, even before the birth pains come. In a moment, just as Israel's anguish starts, the baby is born; the nation begins."

This prophecy was fulfilled in May of 1948 when it was officially declared an independent state. They can hate all they want, but what God has declared is the final word. What He opens no one can shut, and what He closes no one can open.

The day is coming when Russia, Hamas, Iran, Turkey and many other nations will come against Israel, but God will give them the victory. Your fighting and war isn't against them, but against Almighty God, you and your armies are as weak as water fighting against Him.

So while they were talking all this out there came a knock at the door. It was the king's Chamberlains, that had come to Haman's house to escort him to the Queens Banquet. I would say that from all the embarrassment that had taken place that day, he probably forgot all about it. But this was also a custom

6: God Reveals His Plan with a Sense of Humor

in the East for honored guest to be escorted to a dinner. They were given the red-carpet treatment, treated like royalty.

Things are starting to get bad for Haman, because God has stepped in. Let me ask you a question, "Has things gone from bad to worse for you lately?" Maybe you are a Christian and you walked away from God, for some unknown reason. Maybe you've made a mess of things, and God is using these things to correct you and bring you back into the fold.

Maybe you're not a Christian, but God has allowed bad things to come into your life to get your attention. For one reason or another you just brush it off, but things keep getting out of hand. You have had family, friends, co-workers talk to you about accepting Christ as Lord and Savior of your life but you just brush it off. I pray that you will accept Him before it is to late. What I mean by this is to die without Christ it is then to late, because hell will be your home for all eternity. Or if you are still living after the rapture of the church without Christ, once again you will experience a life of hell here on this earth. Because after the Church is gone, you think things are bad now, you haven't seen anything yet. It's not to late to accept Him today. I pray you will.

J. Thomas Ruble II

7

Last Meal, Sudden Death

Verses 1-2

So the king and Haman went to dine with Queen Esther.

And on the second day, at the banquet of wine, the king again said to Esther, "What is your petition, Queen Esther?" It shall be granted to you. And what is your request, up to half the kingdom? It shall be done!"

Things are moving rather quickly here. The eunuchs went to escort Haman from his house to the palace for the banquet. Then once he arrives him and the king walk into the banquet room, for part two of the banquet meal.

Haman had come to the first banquet all happy and bragging to his family and friends about having dinner with the royal couple. He then had a gallows built to hang Mordecai on and went to get the permission of the king to do it. But instead of hanging him on the gallows, he had been humiliated by parading Mordecai around on horse back, dressed in royal robes. Then he goes home to complain about the way he had been treated. Then he is escorted to the banquet.

We don't really know for sure about his attitude here after suffering humiliation earlier that day. I don't know this for sure, but this is my belief about what he is going through at this point. I believe he is saying to himself, "Finally, I can forget about what happened earlier because I am going to a second dinner with the king and queen." I would say also that he had bag of very mixed emotion, but going to a second banquet is going to help his sad emotional ego. However, he is totally unware of what is about to take place, and why he has been invited by Queen Esther.

Once again, the king ask Queen Esther again for a third time. "What is your petition? And What is her request?" He tells her that whatever it is, she would be granted, and it will be done for her; no matter what it is she wants. He was going to give it to her up to half of his kingdom.

To me this is sort of a scary thought. The king is giving her a blank check to fill in. He is giving her the royal credit card if you will. That is scary, because she would probably max them both out. This reminds me a funny story about a man who lost his credit card and he never reported it missing. He kept getting a bill and paying them off every time. The credit card company notice that the card had been stolen and found the man who had stolen it. So they called him and asked, "Do you want to close this account and press charges against the man." He told them, "No, let him keep it, because he charges less than my wife does." Now don't get mad, we've got to love one another. Men are just as careless with money and credit cards as well.

But any. This is totally different with Esther. She doesn't care one iota about riches or owning half the kingdom. What matters to her is the well being, welfare, and the life of her people. However, the king knows that there is a pressing matter pressing on her and he is trying to get her to open up about it. You know sometimes within our marriages; life can get rather hectic. Sometimes we get busy with everyday life, and we become to use to the fact that they are always there; and we take each other for granted. When communication fails inside a marriage the marriage will break down. Sometimes we just need to come out and tell each other what's on our minds. Of course, if I used this tactic with my wife, she'd want to go shopping or to yard sales. But I wouldn't have to worry about her spending hundreds or thousands of dollars, because she would get things on the clearance rack.

So now we are about to see Esther do just that. She is about to get everything laid out on the table. And the king is about to find out what has been bothering her.

Verses 3-4

Then Queen Esther answered and said, "If I have found favor in your sight, O king, and if it pleases the king, let my life be given me and my petition, and my people at my request."

7: Last Meal, Sudden Death

"For we have been sold, my people and I, to be destroyed, to be killed and to be annihilated. Had we been sold as male and female slaves, I would have held my tongue, although the enemy could never compensate for the king's loss."

As we'd say in the country, "The cat is out of the bag now!" Esther has found her courage now, knowing that the king has found favor in her; or better yet, he has her back. She knows now that he loves her and that he has the utmost respect for her. Because if you remember he held out the golden scepter to her when he seen her. He could have had her killed for approaching him unannounced, but he didn't. I believe that the king had grown up and had learned a valuable lesson from divorcing Vashti.

Notice what she says here, "Let my life be given me at my petition, and my people at my request." There is nothing and I mean nothing any greater in this life than living. Money, riches, fame, houses, or land is not any greater than the life that God has given us. The life of all beings that God created is a life that is priceless. That even goes for the life of those unborn babies living in their mother's womb, they are priceless. But their life is cut short because our sins, our blindness to God's word.

Her petition to the king is to allow her life to be spared and to live, because her life has been placed on the chopping block, because of Haman's wicked plan. She is now letting the king know also that she is a Jewish woman. Since she is Jewish, that means that her life will be snubbed out because of his plans. Then she makes it known to the king that she identifies herself with her people. So she is asking him to allow them to live as well. Notice the choice of words that she uses here: We have been sold, her people and herself, to be destroyed, killed, and annihilated. This plan was a plan of genocide against the people of Israel. Now who else do you think is behind this plan. That's right the devil is behind this plan, and Haman is patsy and little puppet to carry out this plan. Because if the entire race of the Jews is annihilated, then the Messiah will not come.

If you remember, back in Matthew Chapter two. After Jesus was born, we find Him, Mary His mother, and Joseph in a house; they are no longer in the stable. The wise men from the East had seen His Star and had come to worship Him. Before they arrived at the house where they were, they stop in Jerusalem at King Herod's palace. They told him that they had come to worship the New

Born King of the Jews. Well that didn't set well with King Herod at all, a King, another King, I'm the King and no one else with me.

He gathered all the chief scribes and scribes of the people together to find out where the Christ was to be born. So they told him, "In Bethlehem of Judea, for thus it is written by the prophet;

"But you, Bethlehem, in the land of Judah, are not the least among the rulers of Judah; For out of you shall come a Ruler Who will shepherd My people Israel."

This prophecy came from Micah, in Micah 5:2 NKJV. But after hearing this, King Herod had a secret meeting with the wise men, to find out when they had first seen the star. So now he knows how long they had seen the star and he knows where Jesus had been born. What's he do next? He sends them on their way to find Jesus so he can go and worship Him too. Is that what he really wanted to do? No! He was wanting them to find out where he was so that he could kill Jesus, because they had called Him King of the Jews. He is jealous and no one else is going to be king except for himself. He had even murdered his own family members.

Being divinely warned in a dream that night they did not return to King Herod. So, they left another to return to their own country. Then Joseph had been warned in a dream to take Jesus and His mother to Egypt. But then King Herod realized that he had been deceived by the wise men, he was furious and sent men to Bethlehem to murder all the newborn males to the age of two years old.

Was this just King Herod, wanting to do this. No, this was none other than the work of the devil to get rid of Jesus. But God wasn't going to allow this to happen so He protected His Son from being killed as an infant, which would have been premature. Because the way that Jesus had to die was determined before the foundation of the world. Man and his evil schemes is puny, very, very puny, before an Almighty God. Although Esther and her people had been sold out by Haman to be killed, destroyed and annihilated. This would have been the end of the Jews as we know it.

Haman is just a little minion of the devil. Just like King Herod tried to have Jesus killed as an infant, and just like Judas betraying Him, the devil thought that would be it when Jesus died. He thought wrong, because even with his limited powers, he could not hold on to the Lamb of God, the King of Kings and Lord of Lords.

If her and her people had been sold as slaves, Esther could have kept quiet about it, because at least then they would have gone on living. But since she and her people were about to be annihilated, she had to speak up for all their lives.

I am reminded of something that B.R. Lakin said one time in a sermon. He was speaking to those who had never accepted Jesus as their Savior and been born again. He said, "You have Someone who votes for you to be saved, and that is Jesus. Then you have someone, the devil vote against you to be saved. That leaves only one person to vote for yourself and that is you. If you vote to accept Jesus then you will be saved."

How often do we ever think about Jesus being our advocate. He does more than just sitting on His throne in heaven. He is all the time praying for us, He is all the time advocating to the Father for us, and He is all the time defending us when our accuser the devil goes before Him pointing his finger of how we slipped up. I must confess that I forget about that sometime.

Verse 5-6

So King Ahasuerus answered and said to Queen Esther, "Who is he and where is he, who would dare presume in his heart to do such a thing?"

And Esther said, "The adversary and enemy is this wicked Haman!" So Haman was terrified before the king and queen.

King Ahasuerus is in a state of shock and in a rage after hearing what Esther had told him. He more less said, "WHAT?" The other problem with him is she told him who it was without naming him and it still hasn't dawned on him who it is. All he knows is that Haman had asked him to bring about the killing of a certain people; and he gave him permission to do it. Haman himself doesn't even know that Esther is a Jew, all he knows is that she is just the queen.

The first thing the king wants to know is who this man is? He didn't know that it was Haman, but Esther knew. The man is right here under your nose and that's why Esther invited him to supper. So King Ahasuerus want to know who would dare do such a thing to his queen. This goes to prove that a man should always, always back his wife up, no matter who it is or what it is. A man and wife are in God's eyes as one person. The man is to treat his wife the way he would treat himself, but better. The husband should always be ready to defend his wife, even if it is family, friends or a stranger. God created them to be a help mate, not to be a punching bag.

Here to I believe that Haman is absolutely clueless as well. I believe he is setting there watching this dialogue taking place with the king and queen. He doesn't know that Esther is Jewish and that his plans have included killing her as well. But what he doesn't realize, he is about to find out; and that his britches is caught on barbwire. Not only that, but his day is about to get worse. He thought is was embarrassing leading Mordecai around on horse back, he hasn't seen anything yet.

Queen Esther has the "Guilty Envelope" in her hands. She breaks open the seal, pulls it out of the envelope, looks at it and reads the name. "O king, the guilty person for this action is none other than our adversary and enemy, this wicked man Haman. She did not pull any punches here. In fact she uses the very strong words here.

Adversary- One that contends with, apposes, or resist.

Enemy- One that is antagonistic to another. Especially one seeking to injure, overthrow, or confound an opponent.

Wicked- Morally very bad: Evil.

(Definitions from Webster Dictionary)

As I said, she pulls no punches. She is not politically correct. She calls it the way she sees it. We need more of this today, instead of allowing the guilty to claim insanity, or some other whishy washy ideology.

Did you notice the words she used here for Haman. The Bible also uses these words for our Adversary, our enemy, and wicked and evil one. Who is the answer to these descriptions? The devil.

1 Peter 5:8 NLT Stay Alert! Watch out for your great enemy the devil. He prowls around like a roaring lion, looking for someone to devour."

He has his army of demons to go out, to seek out and to destroy. His enemy is those of us who profess Jesus Christ as the Son of God and as Lord and

Savior. He does not worry about those he already has. He is out prowling to pounce and to kill Christians. Maybe not so much as killing physically, but to kill us spiritually. He will do things to keep us busy not to pray, read God's Word, go to church, witness, give our tithes and offerings. He will create things to frustrate us in order to ruin our testimony for Jesus. He will do things to create doubt and fear and to give up or not do things for the Lord. Or he will do other things by turning people against us who once were our friends or even family.

Take a good look around us. It's easy to see our enemies are all around us everywhere. They are not only our enemies they are fighting against the Lord as well, because He lives in us and we are apart of Him.

Anyone who take the word of God and denies it as His Word and that it has mistakes in it is an enemy. Anyone who says that God doesn't call sin, sin, is a liar and an enemy. Anyone who says that the birth of Jesus did not happen the way the Bible says and rejects Him as the Christ of God for the sins of the world; is a liar and is an enemy. Anyone who calls sin love, is an enemy.

Jesus said in Luke 9:50 **"But Jesus said to him, Do not forbid him, for he who is not against us is on our side."**

So all those who are from our Federal Government Leaders, State, City, County officials, to all those across this nation. Who stand up in their leadership position to standing in the streets advocating for Abortion, you are a Haman. They believe that it is a woman's right to kill her baby through abortion. Your body just is not your body alone, God created you, it is He Who made you, so your body belongs to Him.

The other Haman's we have in the world are those who believe that homosexuality is love and they can marry, and that God honors it is wrong. Those who believe that God made you a female when you are a male, you are a Haman. Their father, your father is none other than Satan. Bruce Jenner is still Bruce Jenner. There is coming a day when God will bring a final judgement upon the world, and it will be a day that you will not want to experience.

Hebrews 10:31 It is a fearful thing to fall into the hands of the Living God.

Haman is about to meet his fate. I pray that you will not meet your fate before the Lord one day, rejecting Jesus Christ. The judgement of the world is revealed in Revelation. If you think you have it bad now, you haven't seen anything yet.

Verse 7

Then the king arose in his wrath from the banquet of wine and went into the palace garden; but Haman stood before the Queen Esther, pleading for his life, for he saw that evil was determined against him by the king.

The king gets up from the banquet table in a fiery rage and goes into the palace garden. He is so mad that if you touched him with a match, the match would ignite. I believe that he left the room to clear his head to think about just what he has been told. There is a lot of things running through his mind right now. First, I believe that his thoughts are about Esther being killed. Second, I believe that he can't believe that Haman a man that he trusted has brought this about to his wife. I believe too that he now remembers the conversation between him and Haman about killing a certain people. But now it has come home to him, because now his wife the queen is part of that plan of being killed. Last of all, he knows that there is no changing the law, because it is a law of the Medes and Persians; it cannot be changed.

So while he is in the palace garden thinking and cooling off and gathering his thoughts about this. Haman is doing the two step, three step, dos-si-do and tap dancing. I would be willing to say that he had more moves than Frank Sinatra and Ginger Rodgers. This man knows that he is now in serious trouble with the queen and king. Things aren't going the way he planned them to go for this day in his life. First, he is humiliated by leading Mordecai around the city square on horseback, and now he's been found out about killing the queen and her people. He is now pleading for his life, because he knows things have gone sour with him and the king.

Here is a man that hated a man, a Jewish man, for not bowing down to him. But how the tables have turned, because know he is bowing down to a Jewish woman who is queen. He knows how the king is and that he can have him killed at a moments notice. He knows that sudden death is awaiting him just around the corner, and he does not want to die. He is pleading for his life to Queen Esther very hard in order to stay alive.

There will be a lot of people like Haman during the final judgement of God. There are a great deal of people who believe that God is a God of love and not a God of judgement. But the Word of God says otherwise about God, because He is a God of Judgement as well as a God of love. Read Revelation 20:11-15. John seen the dead both small and great standing before God. There were books opened and there was also another book open, this second book was the Book of Life. These who were before God were judge out of the books according to their works.

The sea, death and hell delivered up the dead in them. And everyone of them were judged according to their works. Then everyone of them were cast into the Lake of Fire, this is called the second death. Anyone whose name was not found in the Book of Life was cast into the Lake of Fire.

What this is telling us here is this. The Book of Life is the book of all those who have accepted Christ as the Son of God who died on the cross for their sins, was buried and arose again, who sits at God's right hand on His Throne. Who is one day returning to this earth to conquer Satan, the beast, and the false prophet and all those who follow them. If you have never accepted Christ as Lord and Savior of your life, your name is not written in the Book of Life. Your name is written in the other books of doing good deeds. All of our good works can never measure up to what Christ did on the cross. He shed His blood for us, and gave up His life for us, for you, as if you were the only one to die for. My heart goes out to all those who have chosen to reject Christ and to continue to live in sin, thinking that God will not judge them; even though they performed good deeds and good works. You are going to be defenseless against Almighty God.

Verse 8

When the king returned from the palace garden to the place of the banquet of wine, Haman had fallen across the couch where Esther was. Then the king said, "Will he also assault the queen while I am in the house?" As the word left the king's mouth, they covered Haman's face.

Things have gone from bad to worse for Haman haven't they, but they are about to get worse for him. Because I believe he went stir crazy mad at this point. He was so over come with fear he didn't realize what he was doing. Because he had come upon the couch or here it is called a bed. In the Middle East they reclined on couches when they ate, just like they did in Jesus' day. They would lay on their left side and recline on their left arms, with their feet toward the edge or hanging off the edge of the couch. The beds or couches were not very high but were very wide. One couch or bed could hold up to three or four people at a time. For example: during the Last Supper with Jesus there were probably four of these couches around the table were they ate.

So when the king had returned from the garden, this is where he found Haman. Remember that at first Haman was standing before Queen Esther, but before the king entered back into the room; he threw himself on the bed that she was sitting on. I'd have to say that Haman was innocent here, he is pleading for his life, he is not trying to have his way with her. But! The king does not know that he threw himself at her mercy, all he knows is that he is trying to have his way with her.

The scriptures are silent about the reaction of Esther when he fell upon the couch with her, but I'd say that she had a little fear. Here Haman was pleading for his life, but he took it a step to far. He has now violated the queen's personal space. He shouldn't even be this close to her, with or without the king's presence. So the king sees Haman stretched out on the couch with her and he assumes the worst is taking place. He is thinking that he is already trying to kill Queen Esther while he is in his own house. Unthinkable!

But notice that the word went out of the king's mouth, and they covered Haman's face. Apparently, these bodyguards were in the room while this was taking place. But neither of them moved a muscle while Haman was pouring his heart out to Esther. But as soon as the word came out the kings mouth, they covered his face. This meant he would no longer see the kings face again and also that he was going to be executed.

Everything that Zeresh, Haman's wife and friends had told him was coming to pass. He was going to fall before Mordecai the Jew. They were exactly right; Haman's chickens were coming home to roost. One day, and there is a day coming when the Lord's enemy and our enemy will meet his final doom. One day, the Lord Jesus Christ is going to bound Satan and cast

7: Last Meal, Sudden Death

him into the Lake of Fire. And one day, Jesus is going to bring about the judgement and the end to all the enemies who came against His chosen people Israel. Believe me that day is coming.

Verses 9-10

Now Harbonah one of the eunuchs, said to the king, "Look! The gallows, fifty cubits high, which Haman made for Mordecai, who spoke good on the king's behalf, is standing at the house of Haman." Then the king said, "Hang him on it!"

So they hanged Haman on the gallows that he had prepared for Mordecai. Then the king's wrath subsided.

Just then Harbonah- which means donkey driver speaks up. This man is one of the king's eunuchs, which I believe was probably a close friend of Haman's; and a collaborator in his plans to destroy the Jews. He tells the king about the gallows that Haman had built at his house to hang Mordecai on. He goes on to tell the king about Mordecai and that he was the man who had saved the kings life.

These gallows that Haman had built was built in a garden or a lot that was by his house. These gallows which was built for Mordecai to die on and to bring about satisfaction to the bitterness and hatred Haman had towards Mordecai. Instead of it being the death of a man he despised, was now his own death sentence.

Have you ever noticed through out life how our enemy the devil has laid traps and a gallows for us. He does this through trials, tribulations, heartaches, pain, sickness, etc. He does this in order to trip us up and to cause us to be brought to shame. But Christ takes what is evil and He uses it for our good, so that His name will be praised.

Look at the book of Job and look at how Satan stood before the Lord accusing him. Before he even spoke to the Lord about Job, the Lord knew why he was there. The Lord allowed him to test Job and to bring one disaster upon another upon him. But he was limited to how far he could take each trial, and the one thing the Lord would not allow him to do was to take his life. But in the end, the Lord rewarded Job and blessed him more at the end than at the beginning.

Look at the Life of Jesus while He lived here upon this earth. There were many deceivers other than Judas Iscariot. The other disciples had abandoned Him, Herod the king, Pilot, the religious groups all were evil men, who condemned Jesus to die. God allowed them to have their way with His Son, by slapping Him, hitting Him, spitting on Him, beating Him nearly to death with a whip. He was accused of being a sinner when He never sinned at all and placed on a cross to die as a criminal.

Listen closely to what I am saying. God does not hate People! God hates sin, all sin! Yes, God loved Haman, as well as all everyone who has ever lived including us. He does not want anyone to perish, to die and go to hell. Haman could have changed and came to God and lived, but he refused to follow God, he chose to hate God and to live his life for himself.

The way we know that God loves us and wants what is best for us is found in John 3 and 2 Peter 3.

__John 3:16 "For God so loved the world that He gave His only begotten Son, that whosoever believed in Him should not perish but have everlasting life."__

__2 Peter 3:9 "The Lord is not slack concerning His promise, as some men count slackness; but is longsuffering to us-ward, not willing that any should perish, but that all should come to repentance."__

When it says, "So loved the world," that is not talking about this globe we live on. This is speaking about the People that God has created. If God hated people, it would be a contradiction against Himself, because we are made in his likeness.

Yes, God loves people, He just does not love Christians, He loves sinners as well. He does not just love one group of people; all lives are very important to Him. So He gave His Son Jesus Christ to be our sacrifice for our sins. Jesus canceled our sin debt towards God, He took the punishment that you and I deserved. He wants everyone to be saved, so they will not perish; because He knows the punishment that awaits us, if we refuse to accept Him as Lord and Savior of our lives. To reject Christ as the Son of God, His death, and resurrection seals our fate for ever. To live in total separation from God.

7: Last Meal, Sudden Death

There is a day coming when God will pour out His judgement upon all those who have rejected His Son. Just like Haman meet his doom from the judgement of the king to be hanged on the very gallows he intended to kill Mordecai on. Today we have a choice, either to live for Christ and reign with Him one day for all eternity, or to reject Him and live in hell for all eternity.

J. Thomas Ruble II

8

God's Reversal of Wicked Plans

Verses 1-2

On that day King Ahasuerus gave Queen Esther the house of Haman, the enemy of the Jews. And Mordecai came before the king, for Esther had told how he was related to her.

So the king took off his signet ring, which he had taken from Haman, and gave it to Mordecai; and Esther appointed Mordecai over the house of Haman.

The very same day they hung Haman on the gallows, King Ahasuerus gave Esther everything that Haman owned. He gave her his entire estate because he was a criminal and died a criminal's death. The property was not given to Haman's family, it was given to Esther because the king confiscated it from Haman. Everything Haman had worked for was no longer his or his families; it now belonged to Esther the Queen.

Now after all of this time Esther finally makes it known to the king that Mordecai was her relative. He was her cousin as well as her adopted father, the man that had raised her. I would imagine that there was now a lot of pressure off her now, knowing the king knew the whole truth about her, her relative Mordecai, her people and that she was Jewish. Now there is no more living a secret life and walking around on eggshells any longer.

But notice that after she tells the king who Mordecai is, the king took off his signet ring and gave it to Mordecai. This is the same ring that Haman had been given to wear. So apparently, Haman was stripped of his position as Prime Minister and wearing the king's signet ring. Now Mordecai is given the signet ring as well as the office of Prime Minister. I would be willing to say that this was the first time that the king and Mordecai had met, each other face to face for the first time. I believe this is a picture of the future for the believer in Jesus Christ. One day, each of us will be before Him face to face and will be rewarded for the things that we did for Christ. One day we will hear these words that Jesus spoke in the Book of Matthew.

Matthew 10:32 "Therefore whoever confesses Me before men, him I will confess before My Father who is in heaven."

Matthew 25:21 "His lord said unto him, well done thou good and faithful servant: thou hast been faithful over a few things, I will make you ruler over many things: enter thou into the joy of the Lord."

The greatest reward that we as believers will have in heaven is being with Jesus Christ our Lord; and to be with Him for all eternity. Jesus Christ suffered very, very much. But He had to go through suffering to gain the highest honor of all, victory over death, hell and the grave.

Last of all. Esther put Mordecai over taking care of the property that she now owned. The king gave her this property of Haman's, its her to do what she wants. So she places Mordecai over this property to attend to its care and well being.

The Bible is silent on the subject of what became of Haman and his family and friends. But with the king confiscating the property, they were probably killed along with him? They could have been placed in jail? Or they where probably banished from the kingdom? I don't know for sure, but I believe that they all were killed along with Haman. Therefore, that is why Queen Esther now owned everything that Haman owned.

Verse 3

Now Esther spoke again to the king, fell down at his feet, and implored him with tears to counteract the evil of Haman the Agagite, and the scheme which he had devised against the Jews.

Haman was dead! But the plans of Haman were still very much alive and valid. The reason why is because it was the law of the Medes and Persians. Once it was a law it could not be changed, not evern the king himself could not change it.

Esther comes before the king knowing this. Her heart is broken because the law is still in the effect. She falls down before him with tears in her eyes for her people. So she comes to him for help and looking for ways to put a end of her people being destroyed.

How many times have our hearts been broken, fallen down on our knees before God, pouring out our hearts for a fallen world, as well as our nation. How that we all, all at once would come together in prayer for those who are lost to be saved, that abortion would come to an end, that hatred and bigotry would be brought to an end, and that marriage between homosexuals would be brought to an end.

How great it would be if we all had a heart like Esther's. That we would come before the Lord falling at His feet broken hearted over sin and over our sins. Beseeching Him with real tears from a broken heart because the shape our nation is in. If we did do this, it would change history and be earth moving. How do I know this? Because I believe in Jesus, and I take Him at His very word. He cannot lie, He has never lied, He will never lie.

Jesus said in Mark 11:22-24:

> ***Then Jesus said to His disciples, "Have faith in God. I tell you the truth you can say to this mountain, may you be lifted up and thrown into the sea and it will happen. But you must really believe it will happen and have no doubt in your heart. I tell you, you can pray for anything and if you believe that you received it, it will be yours."***

God can do anything, anytime, anywhere! Jesus said it here in the scripture, that anything can be done, but we must believe that He can do it. He created this world by the speaking of His lips, He spoke it and it came into being. What a awesome, wonderful and amazing God we serve.

Verses 4-6

And the king held out the golden scepter toward Esther. So Esther arose and stood before the king,

And said, "If it pleases the king and if I have found favor in his sight and the thing seems right to the king and I am pleasing in his

eyes, let it be written to revoke the letters devised by Haman, the son of Hammedatha the Agagite, which he wrote to annihilate the Jews who are in all the kings provinces.

"For how can I endure to see the evil that will come to my people? Or how can I endure to see the destruction of my countrymen?"

Once again, the king holds out his golden scepter to Queen Esther. She stayed prostrated to him until he held that scepter out to her. She then knew that it was the right time for her to approach him. So she picked herself up and stood before him. Just as she did this, she said to him again, "If it pleases the king, and if I have found favor in his sight and the thing seems right to the king and I am pleasing in his eyes, let it be written to revoke the letters devised by Haman, the son of Hammedatha the Agagite, which he wrote to annihilate the Jews, who are in all the king's provinces."

Once again, she is wanting to know that the king is on her side, and that he still finds favor in her. If so she is wanting him to allow them to write letters to revoke or in other words to repeal the old decree by writing a new one.

I believe that this weighed heavy on Queens Esther's heart, of having all her people destroyed or as the Bible says, annihilated. In other words, Haman's decree was going to bring an end to Jews, there would be no more Jews living in Israel or throughout the king's entire province. This was very painful, so painful that she could not endure to see it to come to pass, as well as even thinking about it.

This would be like us today, who love our nation. It would pain us as well knowing that someone inside our boundaries as well as outside our boundaries had plans of wiping the United States off the map. None of us would want to see anything like this happen to our countrymen at all.

Think of the pain that Esther is enduring here. The Word of God is silent about, her crying, or having tears in her eyes. But I believe that she was crying, and shedding tears for her people. It wasn't a crying act to play on his sympathy, but actual tears from a broken heart.

When is the last time that we have had a broken heart, for our nation, for other nation's who have spent decades living with genocide? What about having a broken heart and weeping over the countless unborn babies murdered in cold blood through abortion? What about the young women, girls and boys, who have been abducted and sold to become slaves in other countries?

Verses 7-8

Then King Ahasuerus said to Queen Esther and Mordecai the Jew, "Indeed, I have given Esther the house of Haman, and they have hanged him on the gallows because he tried to lay his hand on the Jews.

You yourselves write a decree concerning the Jews, as you please, in the king's name, and seal it with the king's signet ring; for whatever is written in the king's name and sealed with the king's signet ring no one can revoke."

Let's go to Daniel 6 and read verses 8,12 and 15.

Daniel 6:8,12&15

Now O king, establish the decree and sign the writing, so that it cannot be changed, according to the law of the Medes and Persians, which does not alter.

And they went before the king and spoke concerning the king's decree; "Have you not signed a decree that every man who petitions any god or man within thirty days, except you, O king, shall be cast into the den of lions?" The king answered and said, "The thing is true, according to the law of the Medes and Persians, which does not alter."

Then these men approached the king and said to the king, "Know, O king, that it is the law of the Medes and Persians that no decree or statute which the king establishes may be changed."

I choose these scriptures to give us the jest of the laws of the Medes and Persians. Once that law or decree was made into law it was law, there was no changing it. Why? Because they were not from Washington D.C. They were not polished career politicians who changes laws more than we change our socks and shoes. Once it was made a decree, it was chiseled in stone, no turning back.

So we see that the king is speaking to both Queen Esther and Mordecai here. He tells them both, that everything that Haman had was now in the hands of Esther. They reason that he has given everything over to her is because he tried to lay his hand on the Jews. I believe that he had realized that this plan was underhanded, because Haman had tried to pull the wool over his eyes.

So now the king has given them the authority to write a decree, just not a decree but their own decree in how to counterattack the old decree. He gives them his blessing in writing this decree, to write it in his name, place his seal of signet ring on it. Because whatever they write is as good as written by the king himself and no one, and he means no one can revoke it.

With great power comes great responsibility and authority. Jesus Christ had been given great power and authority after His death, burial and resurrection Matthew 28:18. Then He delegated this same authority to His disciples to go out and make disciples as He did. He gave them the authority to baptize in the name of the Father, the Son, and the Holy Spirit. This same authority He gave them He has given to us as well, who are born again.

Luke 10:19 NLT "Look I have given you authority over all the power of the enemy and you can walk among snakes and scorpions and crush them. Nothing will injure you."

Mark 16:15-20 "He gave them the authority and power to baptize. To cast out demons, speak with new tongues, take up serpents, drink poison these things would not hurt them. Laying hands on sick and being healed."

Notice here that in Luke and Mark it speaks of snakes and scorpions. I believe this is talking more of the devil and his demons. But also I believe it says to us for the physical as well. More spiritually than physical, let me explain.

Paul the Apostle was snake bit while putting a arm load of wood on a fire, in Acts 28:3. This snake was deadly poison. When it felt the heat, it bit him on the hand. They were waiting for Paul to fall over dead, but he didn't. Then being human they thought that he was a god.

I believe these promises with all my heart. The reason I do is because the Lord has given me His divine protection from the very same thing. I don't like snakes, I hate them. The only good snake is a dead snake in my book. However, with that said, God did not intend for us to have church to were we handle snakes. That is just dumb! That is not faith.

Now I wasn't bit by a snake, but I was less than a quarter of a inch from a rattle snake. It was stretched out and was not coiled up, which was in my favor. I was so petrified that I couldn't move at all. I stood there like a statute. Then I noticed the snake starting to move, so I slowly backed away from it then took off running. I learned later on from a sergeant I was with, that if it had been coiled up it would have bitten me. I believe that was divine protection from the Lord Himself.

Verses 9-14

So the king's scribes were called at that time, in the third month, which is the month of Sivan, on the twenty-third day; and it was written according to all that Mordecai commanded, to the Jews, the satraps, the governors, and the princes of the provinces from India to Ethiopia, on hundred and twenty-seven provinces in all, to every province in its own script, to every people in their own language, and to the Jews in their own script and language.

And he wrote in the name of King Ahasuerus, sealed it with the king's signet ring, and sent letters by couriers on horseback, riding on royal horses bred from swift steeds.

By these letters the king permitted the Jews who were in every city to gather together and protect their lives-to destroy, kill and annihilate all the forces of any people or province that would assault them, both little children and women, and to plunder their possessions,

On one day in all the provinces of King Ahasuerus, on the thirteenth day of the twelfth month, which is the month Adar.

A copy of the document was to be issued as a decree in every province and published for all people, so that the Jews would be ready on that day to avenge themselves on their enemies.

The couriers who rode on royal horses went out, hastened and pressed on by the king's command. And the decree was issued in Shushan the citadel.

Once again, the king's scribes were called in to write a new edict. This took place in the month of Sivan- meaning- "Season; time" This month is the ninth month of the civil year and the third month of the ecclesiastical year on the Hebrew Calendar. This month has thirty days, and it falls in May-June on Gregorian Calendar. (from Wikipedia)

Before going on let me give you a brief history on the month of Sivan. Information is from Wikipedia.

The 4th of Sivan 1040 B.C. was the birth of King David. He died on the 6th of Sivan 940 B.C.

Also, on the 6th of Sivan 1313 B.C. The Torah was given to Moses at Mount Sinai and thus observed as the holiday Shavuot.

Now here on the 23rd day of Sivan; Mordecai and Esther were sending out letters to all the Jews in the one hundred and twenty-seven provinces. The reason for doing this was to prepare them to defend themselves and their families against the evil plans of Haman, to have them killed.

These letters were also sent to everyone in their written language and the language they spoke. It was also sent to all the ruling officials of each province. Before the Jews did not know and had to learn of their demise second hand. Not this time, this time they are made aware of it and now can take action against the old edict by Haman.

Then we see that Mordecai was now using the power that had been granted to him by King Ahasuerus. Haman had abused this power given to him for evil, but Mordecai was using it for good for his people.

He wrote letters to everyone in the entire province to defend themselves against their enemies. This new edict was binding, because it was written in the king's name and sealed with the king's signet ring. Once this was done it was given to the carriers who rode, horses, mules, camels and young dromedaries. A dromedary is part of the camel family. The only difference between them is a dromedary has one hump and a camel has two humps.

Camel can go up to fifteen days without water and can run about forty miles an hour. A dromedary has been know to carry a rider 115 miles in less than 11 hours. They to can run up to 40 miles per hour over a short distance. (Britannica.com)

We see that they wasted no time getting these letters out to the 127 provinces. They used every animal they had at their disposal.

To me these three verses mean for us today, of getting out the good new of salvation. Jesus is our King; He is the King of King's. His seal upon the believer is the Holy Spirit, and He has given us the power to get His message out to a dying world. A message of hope for the hopeless, a message to bring life to those who are spiritually dead, a message of healing for those who are spiritually sick. We have so many ways of getting out the Gospel today, because Jesus has granted us many ways of doing it.

Look now at verse 11. The king granted the Jews in every city to gather together. Then to take a stand for their lives, for their wives and their children. Then they were to take the spoil of their enemies who rose up against them.

Jesus has given us this authority and power as well. As a church as a whole we should all come together physically, with broken hearts and spirit, fasting and praying together. We should put our sins and differences of opinions behind us; cry out to God to forgive us, for sinning against Him and each other. Then pray for those who are lost and dying and going to hell. I heard Vance Havner say, "Christians, like snowflakes are frail, but when they stick together, they can stop traffic." How true that is.

Don't misconstrued what I am saying here. I am for an uprising, but I am for a spiritual uprising, on our knees, humbling ourselves before Almighty God to turn our nation around. Our fight, our war is not with flesh and blood, (people). Our fight is against Satan and his demons in the world. See Ephesians 6:12.

If we had only pulled together when they took prayer and Bible reading out of schools, our schools would not be a war zone or a shooting gallery. If we had pulled together for the marriage of homosexuals, and having perverted material read to our children in the classroom. Then perverted sinful people wouldn't be going to our schools reading trash to these precious pure minds, telling them that sin is beautiful and right.

But we sit idly by shaking our heads and allowing it take place, instead of pulling together to fight this spiritual battle; through prayer and fasting. We sit around feasting while a dying world is going to hell every second of everyday.

Here the Jews were going to take a stand on the thirteenth day of the month Adar. Now the playing field isn't one sided, it was now on a equal balance. The Jews would be defending themselves against their enemies. The same holds true for them during the tribulation period when the Lord Jesus will defend them. The same hold true for us who are born again. One day the Lord Jesus Christ will bring an end to the reign of Satan once and for all. In the meantime, we must be sharping our swords, taking a stand to fight, to hold the fort until He comes.

This new copy of the new edict was now in writing and was a law of the Medes and Persians. This new edict was hot off the press of the Persian printing press and was going out. The Jews were to be ready to defend themselves and to take everything their enemies owned.

This reminds me of our nation when she was young, and we had what were called Minute Men. These Minute Men were to be ready in a minute's moment to take up arms against the British Army. It also reminds me of the night in Egypt when they had the Passover Meal. They where to have everything on and ready to move out when the Lord commanded them. They were to be ready.

Jesus told us to be ready for when He returns. He told the Parable of the "Ten Virgins," in Matthew 25:1-13. Remember that five of these Virgins were wise and five of them unwise. The five wise Virgins bought oil for their lamps and kept their lamps full, to keep them burning. But the five foolish Virgins did not get oil for their lamps to keep them burning. Their lamps ran out of oil and their lamps went out, so they asked the five wise Virgins to use some of their oil. They refused to give them any because they didn't want to run out of oil either. So the five foolish Virgins went to buy oil to trim their lamps. But while they where gone the Lord came and the door was shut to them and there was no way for them to get in.

What about us? What about you? Are we ready? Are you ready? Those who are ready are those who have accepted Christ as Lord and Savior of their lives. They are reading the scriptures everyday, studying the scriptures, praying over the scriptures, and applying it to their lives daily. Each passing day they struggle with sin, temptation, trials and tribulations, but with the Lords help they carry on.

But then there are those who have rejected Christ and what He did for us on the cross. Each day they continue to live in their sins and believe that they can get to heaven by being good and doing good works. However, there is still hope for them if they are still living, hope that one day before death or the rapture of the church. Because once death comes without Christ all hope is abandoned, there is no hope, just like with the five foolish Virgins. They were shut out, locked out, with no hope.

Verses 15-17

So Mordecai went out from the presence of the king in royal apparel of blue and white, with a great crown of gold and a garment of fine linen and purple; and the city of Shushan rejoiced and was glad.

The Jews had light and gladness, joy and honor.

And in every province and city, wherever the king's command and decree came, the Jews had hoy and gladness, a feast and a holiday. Then many of the people of the land became Jews, because fear of the Jews fell upon them.

Remember that one day Mordecai was wearing sackcloth and ashes. Then for a brief moment he wore the robes and crown of the king. Then he was lead around the citadel on horseback, on a horse the king himself rode on. But now, Mordecai was wearing royal clothing and a crown. His position has changed, his appearance has changed. He was sitting at the king's gate in sackcloth and ashes. Now he is in the presence of the king in the palace and wearing royal apparel and a crown.

This is the same thing that takes place with us before we came to know Christ. We lived in sin sackcloth and ashes. We were separated from God because of our sins. We were miserable sinners. Then through the work of the Holy Spirit we notice that we were wicked sinful people before an Almighty and perfect God. So we turned to the Lord Jesus Christ and believed He was the Son of God who paid our sin debt on the cross, shedding His precious blood for our sins. He cleaned us up, placed royal clothing on us spiritually and a royal crown on us, making us His child.

I believe this is also a picture of the believer when one day, we all will be in the presence of our King. We will be perfect and made complete, given white robe to wear and crowns to wear. That will be the day when Christ comes to get the church in the rapture to make our salvation complete. No more sin, temptation, trials or death.

Then I also believe this is a picture of Christ of how He suffered while on this earth. He was crucified for our sins and suffered physically, spiritually, and emotionally. He said that we to would suffer as He did. But He was raised from the dead and glorified by God the Father. One day to we will be glorified and all the suffering we went trough will be worth it.

Notice the colors that he wore. The Pulpit commentary stated that his was a blue and white stripe garment.

The color blue in the King James Bible is recorded 51 times. The Hebrew word usually translated this color as Tekeleth, which is a reference to the animal from which the dye is obtained.

The color blue can represent God. Read Exodus 24:10;25:3;38:18, Numbers 4:6-12, 2 Chronicles 2:7 and Ezekiel 1:26

It also can represent royalty Esther 1:6; Ezekiel 23:6; Jeremiah 10:9 or riches Ezekiel 27:7,24.

Blue can also mean or symbolize service to God and godly living Exodus 28:6,8,13,31; Numbers 15:38-40; Esther 8:15

The color white is typically associated with purity, things that are good, innocence honesty and cleanliness. White appears in the King James Bible 79 times. It is most frequently mentioned pigment in the New Testament and in the Word of God as a whole. Remember Jesus on the Mount of Transfiguration appeared in a bright white garment.

Gold represents wealth. The Magi brought gold to Jesus when they came to worship Him. The street in heaven are made of pure transparent gold. Our crowns we receive from the Lord are gold. They are pure and do not tarnish.

Purple occurs forty- eight times of which nine are in the New Testament. The Hebrew Old Testament word translated as this color is Argaman. Purple can represent royalty, majesty and high officials, as well as conveying the meaning of wealth, prosperity, and luxury. (Information taken from Bible Study.org)

Hey! We may be poor in earthly wealth. But Jesus has made us more rich than any millionaire or billionaire with heavenly riches. We are rich, and we owe it all to Him.

Notice what the end of verse fifteen says, "and the city of Shushan rejoiced and was glad." Haman had brought about grief, despair, fear turmoil and death. But when people seen Mordecai in his royal apparel it brought life and joy to the entire city. This is what salvation brings with it. King David said, "The king shall joy in thy strength, O Lord and in thy salvation how greatly shall he rejoice."

When we come to the Salvation of the Lord we have something greater than night life, sex, drinking, drugs and parties. There is NOTHING, and I mean nothing can compare to the salvation of the Lord. Salvation is liberating, it is life and the fullness of life. One day the Lord is going to bring about that peace upon the entire world when He returns and cast the devil into the Lake of Fire.

Notice here that the Jews had four things here; they had light, gladness, joy and honor. Jesus Christ is the Light of the world, John 1:1-5; Genesis 1:3. Jesus is that light and His Light brings life, His light dispels the darkness. This is what takes place within us when we accept Him and receive Him into our lives as Lord and Savior. There is no more sin, darkness, and despair, but life and light. We can now see no more to stumble around in the darkness.

Second, they had gladness. Gladness means a feeling or state of well being and contentment. For the Jews as well as those neighbors around them were filled with gladness that an end had come to Haman's wicked plot. This holds true for us when we come to know Jesus Christ. We now have gladness and a sense of gladness in our lives, because He has met our every need. Just as King David wrote in Psalm 23:1 "The Lord is my Shepherd, I shall not want." We become satisfied with Christ and Him alone, because He is all we need.

Some people will say that we're in a state of denial, that we're out of touch with reality; or that our minds are in the clouds. Thank you, but no. We're living the life He called us into. We're no longer carrying that heavy yoke of sin on us no more.

"Come to Me, all you who labor and are heavy laden and I will give you rest. Take my yoke upon you and learn from Me, for I am gentle and lowly of heart, and you will find rest for your souls. For My yoke is easy and my burden is light." Matthew 11:28-30 NKJV.

Does this mean that we ae immune to sin, trouble and sorrows? No! While living in this world, we will have trouble. John 16:33

Third, He is our joy. The biblical definition of joy says that joy is a feeling of good pleasure and happiness; that is dependent on who Jesus is rather than on who we are or what is happing, around us. (justdisciple.com)

Jesus showed us that He is our great example of joy in Mark 4:37-41. He and the disciples were in the boat crossing the Sea of Galilee. While crossing Jesus fell asleep. then all at once a windstorm came up. The disciples were filled with fear and thought they were going to perish. So they awoke Him and told Him, "Don't you care that we are about to sink and perish."

Just then Jesus gets up and tell the sea, "Peace be still!" Next thing you know it was peaceful and calm. Jesus had joy while asleep in that boat. He knew who He was and to Whom He belonged. The disciples did not have joy because they panicked and were filled with fear.

The Apostle Paul had this joy. He had been beaten, stoned, shipwrecked and put into prison. But his joy remained because he kept his eyes on Christ, Who was his joy and not the circumstances he was in.

Fourth is honor. This means a goo reputation and respect. The world around us watches us day in and day out. They knew who we were before coming to Christ and will soon take notice of the change in our lives. There will be those who didn't know us before Christ but knew us after coming to know Him.

They will notice that there is a difference in us, because we don't talk like them, or gossip like them, brag about drinking and getting drunk. We will soon be honored by some of them. Because they will tell others to watch how they talk around us and to be more reverent towards us when we have to work around them on our jobs. This doesn't happen to us all, because to some they could care less if they hurt our feelings or not.

I'll never forget the time that this happened to me at a factory I worked at. This one young girl told this young man, "Why can't you and the other guys be more like him?" She was referring to me. I was like oh no she's went and

8: God's Reversal of Wicked Plans

started something. Next thing I knew, everyone at the table working with us was looking at me. This one guy made a few vulgar remarks about me. Then all at once she asks, "What is the difference in you? Your not like these other guys talking about sex and making rude remarks about me." That's when I told her, "The reason why is because I am a Christian! Jesus has changed me." She smiled at me and told the guy next to her that he needed to be more like me. He looked at me sheeplishly, then told me he was sorry.

Jesus received honor that day and He included me in it as well. All the ones who worked at the table with me began to respect me and stopped talking dirty in front of me. The young man who was talking dirty to the young girl never talked that way to her again. He started treating her with more dignity and honor. That young girl later ended up receiving Jesus as her Savior and going to church.

Notice here in verse seventeen, "the Jews had joy and gladness a feast and a good day. One day we are going to have joy and gladness that is unspeakable, while feasting with the Lord. Oh how great that Supper is going to be. I love my wife's cooking, but I believe the meal that Jesus is preparing for us will be the best supper we'll ever eat.

Last of all, notice that many people became Jews that day. They had been a good witness for the Lord. They became Jews and began to practice their religion worshipping the One and Only true God.

What about you my friend/ Are you living in darkness? Are you living without that perfect joy in your life? Are you tired and burdened down with sin and the pleasures of this life? If you are, Jesus Christ is standing there waiting on you to humble yourself, repent of your sins, confess that you are lost and going to hell without Him, that He is God's One and Only Begotten Son and that He died for your sins, was buried and arose again and sets at the right hand of the Father. Today is the day, if only you will believe and receive Him.

J. Thomas Ruble II

9

Great Celebration of the Feast of Purim

Verses 1-2

Now in the twelfth month, that is the month Adar on the thirteenth day of the same when the kings commandment and his decree drew near to be put in execution in the day the enemies of the Jews hoped to have power over them, (though it was turned to the contrary, that the Jew had rule over them that hated them;)

The Jews gathered themselves together in their cities throughout all the province of the King Ahasuerus to lay hand on such as sought their hurt and no man could withstand them; for the fear of them fell upon all the people.

Well D-Day had arrived! This was the day and the month in which Haman's evil plan was to take place. But! It was also when the new law of the king was to take place as well. All the Jews throughout all the provinces were to come together and defend themselves against their enemies. Notice here in the verse and love this part of the verse,

"In the day that the enemies of the Jews hoped to have power over them, (though it was turned to the contrary, that the Jews had rule over them that hated them.")

Isn't this great! Don, you love it! Here are the enemies of the Jews thought that they had the upper hand on the Jews. They were ready to pounce on them just like a cat will pounce on their prey. But the Bible says, "Though it turned to the contrary." What does that mean? That means that the very opposite happened. Instead of their enemies having the upper hand the Jews had the upper hand over their enemies. Why?

Because God intervened! Man never has the last word, God does. God was not done with Israel, and He still isn't done with Israel. If He was finished with Israel back in this time, Jesus Christ would not had been born into the Nation of Israel.

Let me give you an example of how God works. Just recently on June 24, 2022; the Supreme Court in America overturned Roe vs. Wade. For nearly fifty years America has murdered and killed millions of innocent babies who could not defend themselves. All of us who are believers have prayed for years that this would come to a end, and it has. God brought and end to it, and now America can move forward towards the path of righteousness.

We cannot put God in a box. We've got to allow Him to be God. We cannot control Him, He works in His on power and His own time. However, He ask us to be faithful and obedient as we possibly can, and He will do the rest. Often times God may be silent in our walk with Him, but He is always present with us, even in the shadows.

Verses 3-4

And all the rulers of the provinces and lieutenants and the deputies and officers of the king, helped the Jews because the fear of Mordecai fell upon them.

For Mordecai was great in the kings house and his fame went throughout all the provinces: for this man Mordecai waxed greater and greater.

Notice here that the list of the king's rulers helped the Jews, they helped support them. Notice now that they are all part of the king's ruling political figures. Just like those here in America, President, Vice President, House, Senate, Supreme Court, that goes on down the line; to governors, lieutenant governors, their cabinet members all the way down to city and county officials. These people under the king helped defend the Jews and spared their lives.

One of my favorite Bible verses is Proverbs 29:2 NLT:

9: Great Celebration of the Feast of Purim

"When the godly are in authority the people rejoice. But when the wicked rule, the people groan."

Let's be real and honest about this. Our leaders as well as all the world leaders are very much human as we are. They have sin in their lives and they make bad decisions and mistakes just like everyone else living in this world. So God's Word is completely correct when it says, ***"All have sinned and fallen short of the glory of God."*** So that means that no one who has ever lived or living now or will live one day is sinful by nature. But our leaders and world leaders rule the best way they know how. The problem is that some are just wicked, and they stand for sin.

I believe that Mordecai is a righteous man, he's not perfect but righteous. God was with this man and He walked with him and guided him. That is why the fear of Mordecai fell upon the people is because God was living in and through this man. They had great respect for him as well as for the Jews.

America today as we know it is groaning! America today as we know it is Spiritual dead! Why? Because our leaders do not defend our rights by God's written laws, commands and His written word to us. I'm not just talking about political leaders here, I'm speaking about spiritual leaders as well. They defend those who are guilty of sin and crime. They permit the killing of unborn babies, allow marriage of homosexuals, when they should not be supporting sin.

The One True King is Jesus Christ, the Son of the Living God. He is the leader of all leaders and of All mankind. One day He will be coming back to set things in order, and to judge everyone. First will be the day of judgement for the Christians for what we did with Christ and for Christ. Second, will be the day when He will judge sinners, those who denied Him and rejected Him as the sacrifice for our sins; who believed the devils lie that there were other ways to get to heaven. He will expel all sin, all sinners, the devil and all the angels who followed him. Then there will be peace and everlasting life, forever and ever.

Although God is never mentioned in this book, we can see that God's fingerprint and His handwriting throughout the book. Because God is the only One Who could bring about the respect of this man by living it out in his life. Next, the Lord is the One who brought about his fame through out the entire province of the king. And last of all it was the Lord who had made him to grow stronger and stronger.

This is exactly what the Lord wants to do with us. He wants to be part of our lives to increase our faith, to make us spiritually wealthy, for His kingdom that is coming. Unlike some who teach and preach that the Lord wants us to have millions in the bank, five hundred-thousand-dollar home, driving a Cadillac, perfect health without having a sniffle or head cold. This world is not our home, heaven is our home. Jesus wants us to have a fulfilling rich spiritual life that we lost in the Garden of Eden. Rich in faith, love, joy, peace

Jesus tells us in John 10:10:

"The thief comes only to steal and kill and destroy. I came that they may have life and have it abundantly."

You see this world is not our home, heaven is our home. Jesus wants us to a rich fulfilling spiritual life that we lost in the Garden of Eden because of sin. He wants us to have first of all everlasting life, a life that goes on and on and on forever. A life that never gets sick's or dies. He wants us to be rich in faith, love, joy, peace, longsuffering, kindness, goodness, faithfulness. See Galatians 5:22.

Verses 5-10

Thus the Jews defeat all their enemies with the stroke of the sword, with slaughter and destruction and did what they pleased with those who hated them.

And in Shushan the citadel the Jews killed and destroyed five hundred men.

Also Parshandatha, Dalphon, Aspatha, Paratha, Adalia, Aridatha, Parmashta, Arisai, Aridai, and Vajezatha, the ten sons of Haman the son of Hammedatha, the enemy of the Jews- they killed; but they did not lay a hand on the plunder.

The Jews enemies came out to destroy them. Over five hundred men in the city of Shushan came out to destroy them. Among the five hundred was also the ten sons of Haman. Haman had instilled his hatred for the Jews into his own family. Hate, bitterness and racism is taught in the home first. But the

Jews took up their swords against those who hated them to defend themselves and came out victorious.

Notice that the Jews only concern was in defending the lives of their families and friends. The lives of people were more important than all the wealth that was left behind after the battle. They would not touch one thing these people owned to whom they had killed. They had every right to take it from those who they killed, because the king gave them the right to collect it. But they decided not to because life was more important to them than riches and wealth.

Take a look back at what hate, pride, selfishness and greed has done to other nations in the Bible and throughout history. Take a look back at how it has destroyed our nation in the past and continues to do so today.

Our nation has not recovered from the days of slavery and the Civil War. Our nation still remains splintered and fractured because of prejudice, power and greed. As I have stated before hate and prejudice is taught at home. It seems that this world has a lot more Haman's in it than it does anyone else. Take a good look at what happened to Esau and Jacob. It began before they were even born, they were struggling with each other in Rebekah. Then Esau sold his birthright as the oldest son to Jacob for a bowl of soup. Last of all Jacob and his mother schemed his father to give him, his blessing as the oldest. Esau swore that he would kill Jacob his brother, but Isaac and Rebekah sent him away to her brother Laman to live until Esau's anger had cooled.

Twenty year's later, the two of them meet again face to face. Jacob was scared to death that Esau was going to kill him and those with him. To make sure everything was good between the two of them Jacob sent his brother a very enriching gift of livestock. They meet finally, hugged each other and wept with one another. This was the last time things were this peaceful between the two families. Because later generations wouldn't let it go, they held onto that hate and caused war between them as well as the nation of Edom turning Jews over to their enemies.

Apart from Jesus Christ we can never ever have that deep meaningful love that comes from Him. He is the truest of love.

Verses 11-14

On that day the number of those who were killed in Shushan the citadel was brought to the king.

And the king said to Queen Esther, "The Jews have killed and destroyed five hundred men in Shushan the citadel and the ten sons of Haman. What have they done in the rest of the kings provinces? Now what is your petition? It shall be granted to you. Or what is your further request? It shall be done.

Then Esther said, "If it pleases the king, let it be granted to the Jews who are in Shushan to do again tomorrow according to today's decree and let Haman's ten son's be hanged on the gallows."

So the king commanded this to be done; the decree was issued in Shushan and they hanged Haman's ten sons.

At the end of the day they brought the report of the number of people the Jews had killed on the first day. Upon hearing this report or reading the number of dead in Shushan alone. King Ahasuerus then told Queen Esther the results of the number of men killed that day. He told her that five hundred men had been killed as well as Haman's ten sons. He goes on to tell her that if they had five hundred alone in Shushan what was the number of men who had been killed throughout the entire province. If there had been five hundred men killed in each province of one hundred and twenty-seven province's, that means that 63,500 men had died in one day by the hand of the Jews.

After giving her this report, he wanted to know what else she wanted done. Was this enough? What else need to be done to bring this matter to a close? Whatever she asked for it would be done for her and her people. The king did not want to leave a stone unturned. There was no need to leave thing undone in order for them to have to back and do it all over again days or months later.

So Esther advises that what they've done today, let it also be done the next day as well. The Bible is silent about Mordecai and Esther talking about this, but it is suffice to say that Mordecai was aware of what took place; and was probably making decisions on the matter as well. They probably knew that

9: Great Celebration of the Feast of Purim

there were more men who had not shown their faces the first day, and was laying low for an ambush the next day.

Now let me be clear that Esther is not a blood thirsty woman at all. She wanted to make sure that the purging of all their enemies was made complete. So she tells the king to have the same decree done tomorrow in Shushan just as they had on the first day. Then to have the sons of Haman hanged on the gallows.

The king made a decree that there would be one more day of riding the Jews of their enemies; as well as having Haman's sons hanged on the gallows. With this being done it brought about shame for the house of Haman. Not only that, but this would also place fear into the people that this is what would happen to those who came against them. The same fate would come to them if they thought about carrying out plans to kill all the Jews.

I believe that if Hitler himself had ever read the book of Esther; that it could have brought a fear of God upon him. But if he had read it and simply thought to himself, "This would not happen to me." He realized later that he had brought about this upon himself but never repented of it. Because it had brought about death upon himself, his wife, the nation of Germany; as well as all the other nations who fought against them in World War II.

Verses 15-17

And the Jews who were in Shushan gather together on the fourteenth day of the month Adar and killed three hundred men at Shushan; but they did not lay a hand on the plunder.

The remainder of the Jews in the king's province gather together and protected their lives, had rest from their enemies and killed seventy-five thousand of their enemies; but they did not lay a hand on the plunder.

This was the thirteenth day of the month of Adar. And on the fourteenth of the month they rested and made it a day of feasting and gladness.

The very next day the Jews all gathered together, on the day after the thirteenth which was to be their day of death. But because of what God had done, He gave them a day of victory over their enemies. The next day they had found three hundred more men who held to the plans of Haman. They killed these three hundred men and left the plunder.

This is the second time they did not gather what these men owned. The Pulpit Commentary stated the reason for this, is because they were following after their father of their nation, Abraham. After he rescued his nephew Lot in Genesis 14:21-24. The reason for this is so these people could not say they made them rich. They left everything for the widows and children. If you noticed they had killed only men, not the women and children or the numbers would have been much higher that had been killed. They didn't want riches from evil people, their riches was God and worshipping only Him.

All the Jews in all the provinces of King Ahasuerus reign, gathered together on the thirteenth day which was the day Haman had planned to kill them. They stood up to protect themselves personally, their families, friends and neighbors. When the battle had ended and the smoke cleared. The Jews in all the provinces together had killed seventy-five thousand of their enemies. After this there was peace and the Jews had no need to fear for their lives, they finally had rest, and no more looking over their shoulders. The Jews in the other provinces, did as the Jews had done in Shushan and did not take anything their enemies owned; even though they had been permitted to by the king himself.

The very next day they rested from fear and they celebrated with great joy. They did not strike again as those in Shushan had done. I would say that the reason for this is because what Esther had advised in the king in Shushan was not decreed and sent out to them. They had only carried out what was decreed to them by the carriers to defend themselves just on the thirteenth of the month Adar.

If you notice that there is no mention of the any Jews being killed on this day the thirteenth of Adar. Or any loss of life in Shushan on the thirteenth or the fourteenth. The Word of God gives the total of their enemies that were killed. This tells me that God was the One fighting for them and through them. I would be willing to say that the fear of the Lord came over all the others in the provinces.

God was on Israel's side here, and He is still on Israel's side today. Their enemies live inside the boundaries of their nation as well as outside their nation. But make no mistake about it God will never allow the Nation of Israel

9: Great Celebration of the Feast of Purim

to come to non existence. It does not matter what their enemies think or say God will no allow their enemies to defeat them. Read Psalm Chapter 37

Psalm 37:13 NKJV tells what God does and how He views wicked men.

"The Lord laughs at him, for He sees that his day is coming."

God knows the wickedness of everyone living. He knows that there are some men and women who will never change their ways of living. Their hearts are bent towards evil and wickedness. They think they are a god, they nothing or no one can destroy them. Believe me, I have met people like this and they have actually told me that they are god, that they are in control. They are wrong, eve with all their human strength and power they are ever so weak before Almighty God. How freighting it is to fall into His hands, because we do not stand a chance before Almighty God.

One day man and God are going to have a stand off at the battle of Armageddon. All the armies of the world who are evil and wicked will fight against Jesus and His Army. With all their technology and mastery of weapons, as well as powerful weapons; is no match for Jesus. Because with one small puff of His breath and they'll all be destroyed. We have, we serve an all powerful and almighty God, who can never be destroyed or conquered. I really feel sorry for those who think and believe that there is no God or believe that they can stop Him or defeat Him.

Listen to me and listen good. If all the enemies of God, who came against Him and Israel were completely annihilated. What makes them think they can still come against Him, Israel and His Church and win? They can't! They never will! God will always be victorious. Friend I am reaching out to you to give up, repent of your sins, place your faith in Jesus Christ the Son of God and have victory in this life as well as the life to come.

Verses 18-19

But the Jews who were at Shushan assembled together on the thirteenth day, as well as on the fourteenth; and on the fifteenth of the month they rested, and made it a day of feasting and gladness.

Therefore the Jews of the villages who dwelt in the unwalled towns celebrated the fourteenth day of the month Adar with gladness and feasting, as a holiday, and for sending presents to one another.

The Jews in Shushan carried out killing three hundred more men on the fourteenth day. While they were taking up the loose ends in Shushan. Everyone else was celebrating on the fourteenth day in the unwalled villages as well as the provinces. These unwalled villages were little towns that were outside the city of Shushan in rural areas. Some of the Jewish population lived in these countryside villages. These who lived in these villages were more less farmers, who farmed for a living.

So the Jews who were in Shushan celebrated on the fifteenth of the month of Adar. This was a very joyous time for the Jews, because they had victory over their enemies. This joyous time brought about celebrating and giving gifts to one another. Not only that but they declared this to be a National Holiday for them. This was just not a one-time celebration, but it was to be celebrated through out the years to come.

The month of Adar corresponds to the month of March on Gregorian calendar, which has twenty-nine days. This celebration is known as Purim, which is held every year during this time.

Verses 20-28

And Mordecai wrote these things and sent letters to all the Jews, near and far, who were in all the provinces of King Ahasuerus,

To establish among them that they should celebrate yearly the fourteenth and fifteenth days of the month of Adar,

As the days on which the Jews had rest from their enemies, as the month which was turned from sorrow to joy for them, and from mourning to a holiday; that they should make them days of feasting and joy, of sending presents to one another and gifts to the poor.

So the Jews accepted the custom which they had begun, as Mordecai had written to them,

9: Great Celebration of the Feast of Purim

Because Haman, the son of Hammedatha the Agagite, the enemy of all the Jews, had plotted against the Jews to annihilate them, and had cast Pur (that is, the lot), to consume them and destroy them;

But when Esther came before the king, he commanded by letter that this wicked plot which Haman had devised against the Jews should return on his own head, and that he and his sons should be hanged on the gallows.

So they called these days Purim, after the name Pur. Therefore, because of all the words of this letter, what they had seen concerning this matter and what had happened to them,

The Jews established and imposed it upon themselves and their descendants and all who would join them, that without fail they should celebrate these two days every year, according to the written instructions and according to the prescribed time,

That these days should be remembered and kept throughout every generation, every family, every province, and every city, that these days of Purim should not fail to be observed among the Jews, and that the memory of them should not perish among their descendants.

Mordecai wrote letters to all the Jews from near (Shushan) and far, throughout the villages all the way to Israel, India and all the provinces under the king. These letters he wrote them was to establish these two days the fourteenth and fifteenth should be celebrated every year. Because this was the days that all the Jews had rest from their enemies.

I love the middle part of verse 22, "Which was turned from **sorrow** to **joy** for them, and from **mouring** to a **holiday**; I love this! Their sorrow which was a very deep grief of sadness that they and their families was going to be destroyed. But that sorrow was turned to joy which was a very great thrill of happiness as well as rejoicing. They also went from mourning, wearing sack cloth and ashes as if they were already dead. But their mourning had been turned into a holiday.

I'll never forget the time when I accepted Jesus as my Savior at the age of ten. I rejoiced that I was saved and that Jesus was my Savior as well as my friend. I wanted to know everything about Him and walk close to Him. Not only that, I wanted everyone at church, at school, and those who lived down the road from us that I had accepted Jesus as my Savior. So every year that passed I told everyone that it was my birthday in Jesus.

I remember that our mom and dad would be flabbergasted, every time I told someone about my new birthday. They would tell the people that my birthday was in September not July. I would tell them, "No, that was the day when I was born, but July was when I was born again; my second birthday in Jesus." I couldn't help myself, because I was proud of my new birthday and I celebrated it for several years until I got older; but now I thank the Lord everyday for saving me and making me part of the family of God.

Friends, this could be the day when your sorrow can be turned to joy; and your mourning into a holiday. It's simple! Just acknowledge that you are a sinner apart from the Lord Jesus Christ, and if you died you would be destined for hell. Cry out to Him to forgive you of ALL your sins, confess them to Him and ask Him to come into your life to live. He's right there in front of you waiting to give you a joyous life. There will certainly be rough days ahead of you, but Jesus will see you through everyone of them. He puts everything together when the world around us is falling apart. He will give you gifts to help you to serve Him, but the greatest gift is the gift of the Holy Spirit, Who comes to dwell in you. He will enlighten God's word to you, He will help you grow in Christ each day, He will even help you in praying when you don't know what to pray. He will correct you when you sin, and to move forward in your walk with Christ. My friends, there is no one like Jesus.

So the Jews made this a permanent holiday, for themselves to celebrate every year. Celebrating this yearly is a way of giving God praise and honor for the miracle He had done for His people; for them not being totally destroyed.

This letter that Mordecai had written to all the Jews everywhere became a custom to the Jews. They were to remember how God had saved them from this wicked man Haman, and the evil plot that he had plotted against them. He had cast lots against them in order to bring about the destruction of them all, men, women and children. But this event did not take place because God thwarted this evil man Haman plans, through Mordecai and Esther. They were

9: Great Celebration of the Feast of Purim

to celebrate this day every year throughout the years, of how they had been granted deliverance from this wicked plan.

Each year, we who are Christians celebrate Easter, because that is the day that Jesus died, was buried and Arose again from the grave. Two days earlier He died on a old, rugged cross for our sins, and the sins of the entire world. He died to grant us access to God the Father, because we had separated ourselves from God back in the Garden of Eden. The day that Jesus Arose from that grave, He gave us victory over death and the grave.

I understand that we celebrate it every year, but this is a celebration that should be done each passing day. Because Jesus who was God, died on the cross for us, He was beat and shed His life blood for us to have deliverance over sins, and to have eternal life with Him and the Father.

Just as the Jews turned the tide of being totally destroyed by their enemy Haman. Jesus Christ turned it around on Satan the day He died. Satan thought that he had won the victory because the Son of God was dead. But no! Jesus came out the victor and gave us that victory when we accepted Him as Lord and Savior and Master of our lives. We are not defeated, because through Jesus Christ we are victorious.

The other thing that we should be looking forward to is the return of the Lord. Because when He comes to rapture the church, He is taking us home to be with Him forever more. That means that we will never die, no more suffering trials, tribulations or temptations, it will be over with. The Apostle Paul wrote to the Church in Thessalonica about this in 1 Thessalonians 4:13-18.

The church there was concerned about their loved ones who had died. Paul did not want them to be sorrowful for their loved ones who had died. Their loved ones who had accepted Christ but died, were living with Jesus in heaven. But that there would be a day when Christ would come to get the Church. When He came, they would come with Him, enter their bodies in the grave and come out of the grave, just as He did. Those who were living would be caught up and changed from corruptible bodies into holy bodies. Amen! Amen!

So now it is official, and it is to be celebrated every year, Purim. Purim means lots. They took the Persian word Pur and added the Hebrew Purim to it. This declaration was written and signed by Mordecai the Jew and sealed by the king's ensigna ring. Just as the day we celebrate here in America, "Independence Day." That is the day that America had won her Independence from England. The Jews had won their freedom of being destroyed as a nation, from Haman and those who stood with him.

Purim is celebrated in March. This is when the Book of Esther is read on the first day. During the reading of Esther when Haman's names is mentioned there is a loud noise performed by the people to drown out his name, then they spit; because he is cursed.

They give gifts to one another, especially to the poor. Then they eat triangle shaped food's that is pastries, which is a wildly held tradition. Some believe that it represents Haman's three-cornered hat while others say it represents his ears. Either way they're delicious and eating them represents abolishing the evil associated with the Anti-Jewish prime minister. (Article from National Today.)

There is also symbols for Purim that are called Graggers. Graggers (wooden noisemakers) are symbolic of Purim. Graggers are often made of wood and consist of a handle fixed to a cogged wheel. The cogs on the wheel taps a thin piece of wood fixed to the handle, when the gragger is spun around.

Graggers are used to block out the name of Haman, or the "name of evil," during the reading of the Megilla, also known as the Book of Esther, on Purim. However, anything that makes a loud noise can be used and in some services, people stamp their feet loudly instead.

Other Purim symbols include gift- wrapped food and snacks for friends and the poor as well as puppets used to act out the story of Esther for Children. (from Time and Date)

I liked the part about the three-cornered hat or his ears was shaped like that. I had to laugh, because either way he would have been a funny looking man.

All the articles I found online also stated that they also dress up as the Characters in Esther; to celebrate this occasion. Then the Book of Esther is read again on the last day.

I have noticed by reading the Bible, different articles from news outlets, and seeing it on the news from time to time as a kid, until now. That the Jews are a people who have always had it rough and has been mistreated more than anyone on earth. But the one thing I admire about them is this; they do not whimper, whine or complain about how they are treated; they embrace it and celebrate it.

God has not cast them off as some people think or believe. Today they are back in their land and God has caused them to be prosperous by leaps and bounds. God Bless Israel and God's many blessings be upon His people Israel and peace upon Jerusalem.

Verses 29-32

Then Queen Esther the daughter of Abihail, with Mordecai the Jew wrote with full authority to confirm this second letter about Purim.

And Mordecai sent letters to all the Jews, to the one hundred and twenty-seven provinces of the kingdom of Ahasuerus, with words of peace and truth.

To confirm these days of Purim at their appointed time, as Mordecai the Jew and Queen Esther had prescribed for them, as they had decreed for themselves and their descendants concerning matters of their fasting and lamenting.

So the decree of Esther confirmed these matters of Purim and it was written in the book.

Notice here that verse twenty-nine mentions that Queen Esther is the daughter of Abihail, her real father, then Mordecai the Jew, who adopted her as his own daughter. This is Esther doing the writing here in a second letter to the Jews throughout the provinces. Queen Esther is showing respect and honor to her real father although he has died. She is also mentioning him to let all the other Jews know who her real father is, because a lot of them would probably have known him, and that he had died. Then she mentions Mordecai the Jew as her father or guardian who adopted her and raised her. She is obeying the fifth commandment, to honor your father and mother, that your days may be long upon the land which the Lord thy God giveth thee.

She wrote this letter with full authority. This means with all the power that she had as Queen of Persia. She was writing this letter to confirm or to make known the truthfulness of the second letter that Purim had been set in place as a National Holiday for the Jews and for them to celebrate it every year on the fourteenth and fifteenth of the month of Adar.

Esther and Mordecai did not want this day of Purim to be something half hearted with the Jews. They wanted them all throughout the entire 127 provinces to know that this is to be celebrated year after year; from generation to generation. It is now chiseled in stone. This is now a holiday for all the Jews to celebrate what began as weeping, wailing, and fasting, was now to be a time of celebrating and rejoicing of how God had saved them.

It is now official, Purim is a official Jewish Holiday that the Jews must keep and they have. They have celebrated Purim for three thousand years or more. God Bless the Jews, God bless Israel, God Bless Jerusalem. But most of all praise and glory to the God and Savior of Israel for bringing peace to His people and this great celebration.

10

Peace & Prosperity

Verses 1-3

And King Ahasuerus imposed tribute on the land and on the islands of the sea.

Now all the acts of his power and his might and the account of the greatness of Mordecai, to which the king advanced him are they not written in the book of the chronicles of the kings of Media and Persia?

For Mordecai the Jew was second to King Ahasuerus and was great among the Jews and well received by the multitude of his brethren, seeking the good of his people and speaking peace to all his countrymen.

    King Ahasuerus here imposes a tribute on the provinces and islands. This tribute is none other than a heavy tax that the people had to pay to him. I would say that his money coffers were running low, because of fighting against Greece that he lost, the party that he had back in chapter one, the party that he had for Queen Esther becoming queen, giving Haman money to wipe out the Jews, then for the decree to be sent out to the Jews throughout his kingdom to protect themselves.

    Since the Jews did not take anything pertaining to what was left from their enemies, everything probably went to him. So he imposed a heavy tax upon the people to keep things going but also for his own personal use. But I did learn that he did a lot of major building of things. King Darius had left a lot of projects undone, that he had wanted to build. In 465 B.C., King Ahasuerus was assassinated by Artabanus, the commander of the royal bodyguard.

But most of everything that he and Mordecai had done; had been written in the books of the Meds and Persians. Most articles I read on this stated that those books were long lost. But there is a contrast between these two men.

Both of them had power. The only difference was that King Ahasuerus had wealth and gained it by taxing the people. You make enemies doing that. Mordecai on the other hand was a humble man, one who feared God. Yes, he had material wealth. But the greatest wealth he had was he was great among his people, and greatly honored and loved by his people. He loved them and served them and spoke peaceable things to his people. He was far greater and richer than King Ahasuerus was. God exalts those who are humble and He humbles those who exalts themselves.

When the life of a man or a woman is in direct line with the Lord; He puts everything in perfect balance. Why? Because Jesus has everything in control, He put everything in perspective, He balances everything out in our lives even when chaos is all around us.

Mordecai came to Babylon as a slave, but God took the situation he was in and made him the Prime Minister of Persia. So you think God can't us you? Try Him and He will prove you wrong every time. Because God is always with us, even when He stands in the shadows.

Queen Esther became the mother of King Darius II, also known by his given name Ochus, King of the Achaemenid Empire from 423 to 405 or 404 B.C. According to one tradition, she was forty years old, while another places her age at seventy-four which is the numerical value of the name "Hadassah." (information from jwa.org) The Bible is silent on her age as well as the age of Mordecai and how they died. But it is likely that when King Ahasuerus was assassinated that they could have been as well.

Although the Book of Esther never mentions the name of God, we can see that God's fingerprints are all over this book. God took a young Jewish girl to be the wife and Queen of King Ahasuerus to save her people. Even though the odds were against them and everything seemed very impossible of overcoming. With God all things are possible.

Things seem to be impossible in our nation and around the world, but there is a day coming, when our Lord and King will arrive to set things in order. He will reward us for our faithfulness, being obedient, and placing our complete trust in Him. There are a lot of shadows of uncertainties in our days and time just like there was for Esther, Mordecai and their people. But let's not forget that our God and King is watching from the shadows, keeping His eye on us day and night. Nothing, can ever hurt us unless He allows it. He allows trials, tribulations and temptations in our lives in order to make us more into the likeness of His Son Jesus Christ. Let us band together, pray for one another and help one another.

J. Thomas Ruble II

For author interviews or more information contact:

J. Thomas Ruble II
C/O Advantage Books
info@advbooks.com

To purchase additional copies of these books, visit our bookstore at
www.advbookstore.com

Orlando, Florida, USA
"we bring dreams to life"™
www.advbookstore.com